MASTER OF THE CALCULATED RISK

JAMES H. "JIMMY" DOOLITTLE

A Pictorial Biography

by Carroll V. Glines

Pictorial Histories Publishing Co, Inc.
Missoula, Montana

LIBRARY OF CONGRESS
CONTROL NUMBER 2002104402

ISBN 1-57510-096-7

Printed in Canada

Cover Design and Graphics: Mike Egeler, Egeler Design
Layout Design: Stan Cohen
Typography: Leslie Maricelli

PICTORIAL HISTORIES PUBLISHING CO., INC.
713 South Third West, Missoula, Montana 59801
Website - pictorialhistoriespublishing.com
E-mail - john@pictorialhistoriespublishing.com
Phone (406) 549-8488 Fax (406) 728-9280

Introduction

I have followed the lives of two of America's greatest airmen - Charles A. Lindbergh and James H. "Jimmy" Doolittle - since my elementary school days. I met the former briefly in Germany during the Berlin Airlift in 1948 and was impressed with his easy manner and cordiality. I took motion pictures of him that day which I value very highly.

My introduction to Jimmy Doolittle took place at a reunion of his Tokyo Raiders in 1962. They had been looking for a writer to do a book about their epic air mission of 1942 and I volunteered. The only book about the raid by that time had been Ted Lawson's personal story, *Thirty Seconds over Tokyo*. Jimmy promised his wholehearted cooperation and *Doolittle's Tokyo Raiders* was published in 1964. This was followed two years later at their request by the poignant story titled *Four Came Home* about his eight Raiders who had been captured and treated so cruelly by the Japanese. I have been privileged to be invited to all Raider reunions since as their Historian.

I wrote a biography about Jimmy under the title of *Jimmy Doolittle: Daredevil Aviator and Scientist* in 1972. I asked him if he would consider an autobiography but he declined because he thought an autobiography was too self-serving. However, in 1989, his family contacted me and said he was then ready to tell his life story; thus began a close association that I value as one of the high points of my writing life. His personal life story was published in 1991 under the title *I Could Never Be So Lucky Again*. He was a completely candid and honest subject in his recall of people and events but would not comment if his memory failed him. Mrs. "Joe" Doolittle had preserved much of the personal correspondence between them and he also had extensive files that helped fill in any memory gaps. I also received complete cooperation from the Air Force and his former business associates whenever I asked for information. Especially valuable were the scrapbooks and photo albums the Doolittle's had sent to the Air Force Academy and the Library of Congress.

This book is meant to be a pictorial supplement to those works and further relate and illustrate the active life of a man who made aerospace history in so many ways. His wise counsel would be particularly valuable and insightful if he were with us in these trying times today. He was the right man for his time. His kind will not come this way again.

Carroll V. Glines
Colonel, USAF (Ret.)

I first got involved with the Doolittle Raiders in 1983 when I published my pictorial history of the raid - *Destination Toyko*. This was partly due to the fact that one of the raiders, Dave Thatcher lives in my hometown of Missoula, Montana. It has been my great pleasure to be associated with the Raiders for the past 19 years, to work with the author on this book and to have published his book, *Four Came Home,* on the raiders imprisoned in China. It was also a great thrill for me to have known Jimmy Doolittle for the first few years that I attended the annual reunions. He was truly a hero of World War Two and one of America's greatest aviators.

Stan Cohen
Publisher

CONTENTS

100,000
OTHER YANKS
ARE READY
TO DO WHAT
JIMMY
DOOLITTLE
DID
MERIWETHER
FEB
27
1943
S. C.
WIN THE WAR
3¢
3¢
UNITED STATES POSTAGE
Mrs. Leon A. Thompson
41 Granite Street
Cambridge
Massachusetts

Chapter 1
A Morale Boost for America

It was the best news Americans had received since Japanese planes devastated U.S. naval and air forces at Pearl Harbor, Hawaii, in a surprise attack on December 7, 1941. On April 18, 1942, sixteen American planes bombed Tokyo and four other large cities in Japan in a surprise air raid just as the Japanese had done four and a half months before. The Japanese were furious; American morale soared. Somehow, U.S. bombers had managed to penetrate the enemy defenses, dropped their bombs on military targets and fled to China.

Newspaper headlines around the world screamed: **TOKYO BOMBED!** American aircraft had struck back for "the unprovoked and dastardly attack" that President Roosevelt condemned in a speech before Congress. The details

EXTRA!

9 A.M. FINAL — Los Angeles Times — 9 A.M. FINAL

SATURDAY MORNING, APRIL 18, 1942 — DAILY, FIVE CENTS

TOKYO, KOBE, YOKOHAMA

BOMBED!

were not forthcoming and for a month the public did not know who had led the attack but within hours of its completion, Lt. Col. James H. "Jimmy" Doolittle had been promoted to brigadier general, skipping the rank of colonel. The fact that the attacking planes had been launched from a U.S. aircraft carrier was not released and remained secret for a year.

Sixteen North American B-25 medium bombers with 80 men aboard them had carried out the raid on five Japanese cities. Fifteen planes headed for China and ran into bad weather. Eleven crews, including Doolittle's, bailed out at night over the mountains; four ditched in the ocean off shore or crash-landed near the beach. The pilot of the sixteenth plane, reportedly very short of gas, decided to head for Russia and landed safely near Vladivostok but the plane and crew were promptly interned because Russia officially remained neutral toward Japan. They remained in detention as internees until they escaped 14 months later with the aid of a border runner.

Doolittle and his crew were unharmed from their bailouts and he immediately tried to find out the fate of the other 75 men as most tried to make their way to Chungking, their ultimate destination. When the information about each crew slowly became known, Doolittle was ordered back to the States where it was acknowledged that the trophy-winning racing pilot with the famous grin had indeed led the raid and had provided the biggest morale boost for the Allies in the war

Doolittle's medal of honor is on display at the U.S. Air Force Museum, Dayton, Ohio.

thus far. He was invited to the White House where President Roosevelt awarded him the Medal of Honor, the highest award for bravery in wartime that a grateful nation can bestow on a military person.

Doolittle made a nationwide radio talk that day and described how the raid was conducted:

"We approached our targets flying very fast and very low - just above the treetops - going up to 1,500 feet only to release our bombs on objectives - and then dropping down on the tree-tops again.

"Since we skimmed the tree-tops, we were a very elusive target for anti-aircraft fire. Also, it was very difficult for the Japanese pursuit planes to attack us at such low altitudes. Of course, we ran the danger of machine gun fire from the ground. But we were counting on surprise. And Japan was not thus prepared to meet us. We were gone before they could bring such weapons to bear against us.

"We were gratified that we were able to hit our primary targets and that we had not inadvertently bombed other than military objectives. Before departing, I had been very explicit in this respect. We passed very near the Imperial Palace. It offered an open target. But each crew followed instructions throughout and the damage we inflicted upon the Japanese mainland was military.

"It was a strange sensation to hear the excited voice of the Japanese radio announcer apparently reciting in terror the facts and details of our visit, and at the same time to be able to look down upon the Japanese people and see the startled, almost unbelieving expressions on their faces...The greatest result of our raid is the material and psychological damage we inflicted upon the enemy. In neither respect is the enemy likely to recover soon. The next most gratifying aspect is the security of the brave men who accompanied me on this mission for which they volunteered. They did not seek the path of glory. They merely volunteered for a hazardous mission, knowing full well what such a phrase implied concerning their chances for personal safety. They followed the finest traditions of American fighting men. They were, indeed, the finest fighting men I've ever been associated with."

When the world thus learned who had led the mission, the *Nome Nugget*, the only newspaper in the tiny village of Nome, Alaska, published an issue with the largest headline type available in the print shop bragging that one of their local boys had made history.

It was true. The man who had become world famous as a racing pilot had become an immediate American hero for leading the first strike against Japan. And he had indeed lived in the fabled Gold Rush town of Nome on the Bering Sea and had actually sold the *Nugget* to earn his first pocket money. It was in this isolated village in the Territory of Alaska that this pilot who later became known as the "Master of the Calculated Risk" got his start at age four.

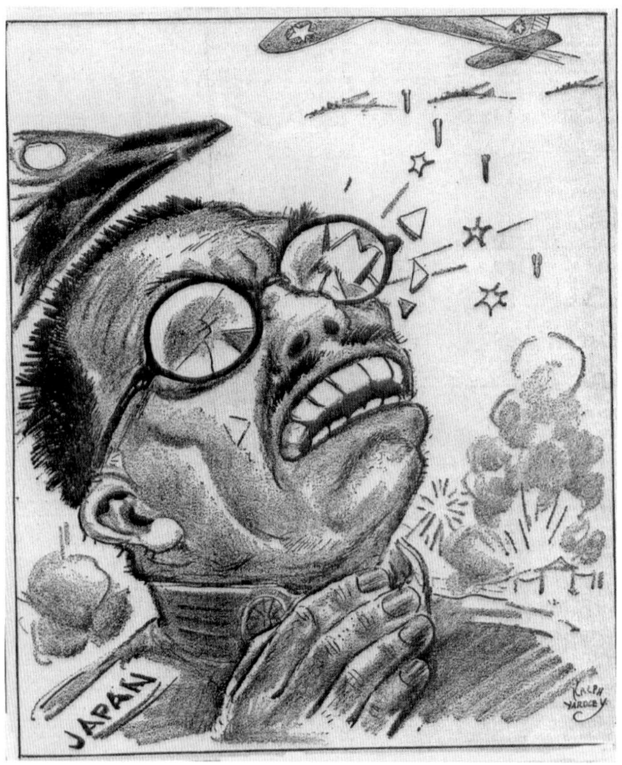

This cartoon appeared in the *Stockton Record Edition* shortly after the attack on Japan. The raid created a great psychological boost for the American people.

Chapter 2
The Lad from Alameda

The lure of gold has captured the minds and souls of men for centuries. When ever it has been discovered, men and women have left families and friends and risked their lives to search for the yellow mineral. The Gold Rush to California in 1849 had been inspired by the discovery of gold at Sutter's Mill. In 1898, there was a rush to the Klondike River area of western Canada when gold was discovered there and along the Yukon River. The rush cooled a year later until there was a report that gold had been discovered on the beach at Nome, a small village on the southern shore of the Seward Peninsula. The report was true. All a person needed was a shovel, a bucket and a rocker box. Within two months of its discovery, 2000 people were at work sifting sand on the beach from which more than $1 million in gold was extracted.

When the gold dust arrived at west coast ports as proof of the strike, an additional 15,000 people reached Nome in 1900. Among them was Frank H. Doolittle, a carpenter who had gone to the Klondike in 1897 and had followed each new rumor down the Yukon River until he reached the sea at Nome. He had left his wife Rosa and son James Harold, born on December 14, 1896, behind in Alameda, California. He sent for them and they arrived by ocean steamer in the summer of 1900.

The scene that awaited them was chaotic. Thousands of people were sleeping outdoors, in tents or shacks along the beach, all intent on sifting the sands for the yellow glint that meant realization of a dream. As the population increased, so did crime. Alaska was then a land without effective government or police. Citizens took the law into their own hands. Despite the almost impossible conditions, Nome survived, streets were laid out which were nothing but muddy trails with board sidewalks. Sanitation was a serious problem and diseases like typhoid, dysentery and pneumonia were common. Law enforcement was difficult and crime increased with the population. Disputes were settled with guns, knives and fists. The lust for gold had attracted not only optimistic adventurers but also gamblers, thieves, confidence men and prostitutes in droves.

Frank Doolittle, a man who had made a living with his carpentry, took advantage of the need that new arrivals had for shelter when winter came and prospered practicing his trade. Wood was scarce but boatloads had arrived in the summer of 1900. He built a house for the three of them and worked long days building them for others who chose to remain.

The Nome gold rush ended in the fall of 1900 as quickly as it had begun. The relentless cold and long nights took their toll and the 25,000 people that had arrived was reduced to 5,000 after the last boat left for the States.

Life was difficult for adults and especially for a young lad who was small for his age. Jimmy Doolittle soon found that bigger boys delighted in taunting him. His first fist fight occurred at age 5 on the beach when he was approached by an

Jimmy Doolittle spent his early years in Nome, Alaska, where his father was a carpenter. This photo was taken in 1902 just before he started first grade. After the first day, he pleaded with his mother to cut the long curls off. A note on the back of the photo said, "Had terrible accident because didn't know one could leave room by raising hand." COURTESY ROBERT C. REEVE

Mrs. Doolittle was an excellent dog sled driver and a good shot with a rifle. She and Jimmy often went hunting and fishing together. She poses before leaving the house that her husband built on Third Avenue in Nome. DOOLITTLE COLLECTION At right, the house as it appears today awaiting possible restoration. ANNE MILLBROOKE PHOTO

Eskimo boy a head taller than Jimmy, who started to push him around. Jimmy pushed back and managed to punch the boy in the nose. Blood gushed down his face and onto his clothes. Frightened, they both stopped fighting; neither had seen human blood before. The boy thought he was dying and quickly ran home to his mother. Jimmy did the same, thinking he had killed an Eskimo.

The word spread quickly. The curly-haired Doolittle kid was small but tough. Bigger boys provoked him into fighting and invariably found out that the little guy quickly drew blood by flailing wildly and aiming at an opponent's nose. By the time he entered first grade, he had earned respect from his peers. Each new grade school kid who arrived in Nome was goaded by the older and taller boys into trying to whip him but soon learned that this undersized terror knew how to take care of himself. He surprised those who tried to push him around by rushing intensively at them early with a flurry of punches until they backed off and gave up. When several boys much larger and taller went home with bloody noses, he earned a measure of respect.

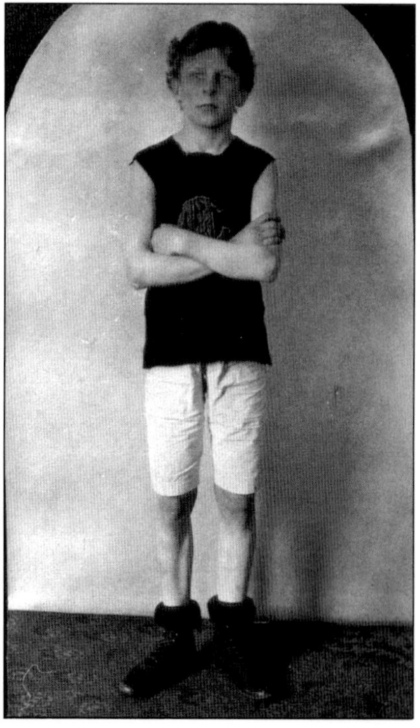

The future racing pilot and military hero took up acrobatics and running in elementary school in Nome. Shorter than his classmates, he often had to defend himself from bigger boys and won a reputation as a fierce opponent who should not be provoked. DOOLITTLE COLLECTION

In the summer of 1904, Jimmy's father took him on a quick trip to Seattle. It was a memorable boat excursion for the seven-year-old and the sights of the big city impressed him. He saw his first automobile, train and trolley car. For the first time, he saw large stores that specialized in selling clothes, groceries and the latest tools. And, remarkably, all the houses had paint on them.

"My values changed right there," he recalled years later. "I saw everything from a new perspective and I wanted very much to be a part of the exciting life I saw so briefly then."

When he returned to Nome, Jimmy got a job selling the *Nome Nugget*, the town's tabloid newspaper, and the Seattle papers when they arrived on the latest steamers. He began to read everything he could find in books, magazines and newspapers about the world he had experienced

Rosa Shepard Doolittle and Frank H. Doolittle with their only child at their home in Nome circa 1908. Mr. Doolittle was an excellent carpenter who had traveled to Alaska to search for gold. DOOLITTLE COLLECTION, AIR FORCE ACADEMY

Jimmy poses casually in his best Sunday suit in front of his home in Nome. DOOLITTLE COLLECTION, AIR FORCE ACADEMY

Mrs. Staples' fourth grade class at Nome Elementary School in 1904. Jimmy is standing at far left. DOOLITTLE COLLECTION, AIR FORCE ACADEMY

so briefly in the world everyone there called "outside." He resolved that when he was old enough he was going to leave the fabled beaches of Nome and seek his fortune elsewhere.

It isn't known what happened between Frank and Rosa Doolittle but Jimmy's mother took him from Nome to California on one of the first boats in the spring of 1908 when he was 11. One of the reasons his father may have stayed was because skilled carpenters could earn as much as a dollar an hour in Nome, while in the States a craftsman rarely made more than 25 cents an hour. However, Frank Doolittle was also inclined to be an adventurer at heart and may have remained in Alaska to follow every subsequent rumor of new gold finds until he died in 1917.

Meanwhile, Jimmy and his mother began a new life in Los Angeles, California where the boy would become a man who would one day be respected and honored for his contributions to aeronautics—a word that was just beginning to apply to "aeroplanes" those motorized gliders that Wilbur and Orville Wright had successfully flown for the first time on December 17, 1903.

Jimmy attended Borendo Grammar School for two years and then enrolled at Los Angeles Manual Arts School in 1910. He didn't have a fondness for academic classes but did have a liking for the shop courses working on gasoline engines and wood lathes. His physical interests turned to tumbling and acrobatics.

It wasn't long before the scrappy kid from Alaska came to be known in his neighborhood for his ability to lick taller and heavier fellows with his wild, swinging punches. Forest Bailey, a teacher, watched Jimmy as he was infuriated at being pushed into a school yard scrap one day at recess and lost his temper. He took Jimmy aside and said, "Look, young fellow, I know a little bit about boxing and you're going to get hurt badly one of these days. You get mad when you fight and if you lose your temper, you're going to get licked sooner or later because you let your emotions rule your body instead of your head. If you really want to learn to box, I'll teach you."

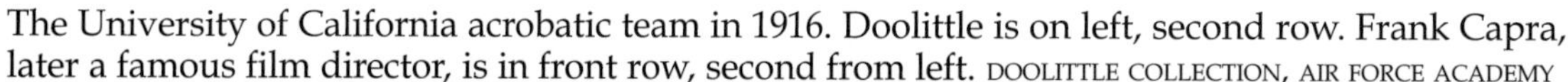

The University of California acrobatic team in 1916. Doolittle is on left, second row. Frank Capra, later a famous film director, is in front row, second from left. DOOLITTLE COLLECTION, AIR FORCE ACADEMY

Mr. Bailey did teach Jimmy how to bob and weave around an opponent until he saw an opportunity to strike the moment the other fellow's guard was down. The instruction paid off. Jimmy entered the Pacific Coast amateur matches in the 105-pound weight class at the Los Angeles Athletic Club. In 1912, at age 15, Jimmy won the West Coast high school amateur championship in the bantam-weight class.

In 1913, he developed a new interest. In January that year in Los Angeles, he attended the first U.S. aviation meet west of the Mississippi River. He watched Glenn Curtiss set a new speed record of 55 miles an hour in a flying machine he had built. Louis Paulhan, a Frenchman, set an altitude mark in his machine of 4,165 feet. Roy Knabenshue and Lincoln Beachey raced each other in dirigibles. These scenes were etched in his memory and he resolved he would try to emulate the men and their frail craft that took them aloft and returned them to earth safely.

He chanced upon an article in an old 1910 copy of *Popular Mechanics* magazine that explained how to make a glider and felt he had to make one for himself. He spent hours in a shed behind his house following the drawings and fashioning spruce wood strips into two wings, covering them with cloth and making a fuselage. When he was ready for a test flight, he carried his creation to a nearby hill thirty feet above the street. He figured that if he ran fast enough to the edge of the hill and leaped off, he would glide to a soft landing below. Instead of soaring, however, the wing collapsed, sending Jimmy to the bottom of the hill amidst a collection of wood, wire and torn cloth. He wasn't hurt but wondered what had gone wrong.

He dragged the wreckage home and began rebuilding it. He decided that more speed was needed for the takeoff and persuaded a friend to get his family car to gain more speed. He attached the glider to the rear bumper and gave his friend the signal to start forward. Jimmy ran behind the car with the glider under his arms and when he thought he had enough speed, leaped into the air. The craft was airborne briefly, then crashed to the ground. The driver couldn't stop very easily and Jimmy was dragged for about a hundred feet. The glider was battered to pieces, his clothes were torn and he suffered cuts and bruises.

He was not discouraged and built another glider based on drawings of the plane with a motor in which Alberto Santos-Dumont had flown to fame in France. For an engine, Jimmy decided to buy a used a motorcycle engine. However, this required money which Jimmy acquired by using his fists in amateur boxing matches in downtown Los Angeles. The promoters gave gold watches to the winners but always bought them back for $10. Jimmy won three bouts and the $30 was enough for an engine.

He quickly went to work on his own version of the Santos-Dumont machine but before he could make his first flight, a thunderstorm slashed through the city. A burst of wind caught the plane in his back yard, lifted it over the fence and smashed it into a neighbor's yard.

Jimmy's mother had not liked the idea of her son boxing or trying to fly. She told him that if he would quit both, she would buy him a motorcycle. He agreed. A junior in high school, he met a pretty girl from Louisiana named Josephine Daniels and tried to impress her. He found that her nickname was spelled "Joe" instead of "Jo" because a favorite uncle was named Joe and family members called her "Little Joe."

Joe did not like the thought of having a boyfriend who seemed like he wanted to fight all the time and told him so. He began to comb his hair, wear a tie, look after his clothes and watched his language around her. He needed money for occasional dates and knew the best way to get it was to box professionally. Unknown to either Joe or his mother, he motorcycled to boxing matches and promoters found that spectators rooted for him because he looked like the underdog because of his size. He either won all of his bouts or boxed to a draw and made as much as $30 a night.

In 1914, after completing high school, Jimmy went to Seward, Alaska and worked with his father building two houses. They didn't get along and Jimmy left to pan for gold. He camped in a tent and subsisted on fish three times a day. He returned to Los Angeles at the end of the summer in 1915 to enter junior college and enroll in the engineering curriculum. He found he liked the math and science courses and enrolled two years later at the University of California School of Mines at Berkeley with a major in mining engineering.

Jimmy liked the academic challenge but the urge for physical combat was strong. He won a slot on the UCLA boxing team by defeating taller opponents who outweighed him. Although a lightweight, he became middleweight champion of the University of California.

In order to make extra money, he began to box professionally under the assumed name of Jimmy Pierce. He won a number of bouts until he met a wing-wise veteran named Spider Kelly who won the fight by a unanimous decision. "It taught me a valuable lesson," Doolittle said. "No matter how good you think you are in a sport, eventually someone will come along who proves that he is better."

A casually dressed Doolittle poses at his home in Alameda, California. He boxed at the University of California, Berkley and was West Coast flyweight and bantam weight champion. He boxed professionally under the name of Jimmy Pierce to earn extra money. DOOLITTLE COLLECTION, AIR FORCE ACADEMY

Chapter 3
A Flier's Career Begins

Although Jimmy Doolittle didn't realize it at the time, he had almost grown up with heavier-than-air flight. On May 6, 1896, a few months before he was born, a small unmanned airplane model flew about a half mile over the Potomac River. On November 26, another flight was made and Dr. Samuel P. Langley, secretary of the Smithsonian Institution was awarded a $50,000 contract by the U.S. War Department to construct one that would carry a pilot. It took five years of experimenting with more models but on October 7, 1903, Charles M. Manly, Langley's mechanic, tried to fly a larger plane catapulted from the top of a houseboat anchored in the river. He nearly drowned but tried again on December 8 and failed again.

On December 17, 1903, three days after Jimmy Doolittle's seventh birthday, two unknown bicycle mechanics from Dayton, Ohio, made history's first sustained, controlled, powered flights in a heavier-than-air machine. Neither had ever studied science or mechanics and had never been to college but had succeeded where others had failed.

When Doolittle was eleven years old, the brothers sold the first aircraft to the U. S. Army and the nation's air force was born. By the time Doolittle was 15 and had experimented with his own glider in 1912, aviation had come a long way. Top speed was 80 miles an hour, the endurance record was 14 hours, an altitude of 13,000 feet had been reached and 12 people had been carried aloft.

Ironically, by the time World War I had begun in Europe in 1914, the United States was far behind several European nations in aviation developments. In the early days of the war, airplanes had been used to detect enemy troop movements, drop bombs and spew bullets from machine guns into ground and air targets. As the months passed, the weapons and planes of France, Germany, England, Russia and Italy improved in speed and flying capability. The United States earmarked only a few thousand dollars for aviation.

A testing ground for American military planes was on the Mexican border in 1916 when the bandit Francisco "Pancho" Villa raided Columbus, New Mexico and killed a number of Americans. The U. S. Army was ordered to send an expedition across the border to chase him down. Included were eight under-powered Curtiss Jennies under the command of Capt. Benjamin D. Foulois. Within a short time, it was apparent the planes were not capable of doing any reconnaissance and were dangerous to fly. It was not until America declared war on Germany in 1917 that the first substantial appropriations were made. Supposedly, the United States could now build thousands of planes and train hundreds of pilots to help the Allies win the war.

American industry went to work trying to meet the demand for military planes and the call went out to the nation's youth to volunteer for service for the army's expanding air arm. Successful applicants were sent to ground schools set up at eight engineering colleges across the country for the study of radio, Morse code, aerial photography, meteorology, map reading, gunnery, aircraft engines and aerial tactics. Upon completion, flying cadets were sent to one of 18 hastily built flying fields constructed for dual instruction, solo practice and cross-country flying.

Even though Doolittle was intent on becoming a mining engineer, he did not ignore what was happening around him. He learned about the exciting flying feats of the British, French, Canadian and German aces and the idea of men fighting in the air alone, pitting their skills against each other thousands of feet in the air, fired his young imagination. He left college without completing his last year and enlisted in the Aviation Section of the Army Signal Corps Reserve in the fall of 1917. He was assigned to take preflight ground training at the University of California, his alma mater.

A dapper Doolittle began to date a young lady named Josephine Daniels, nicknamed "Joe" (always spelled with the "e") who disapproved of his boxing and too-casual dress. Here he wears a fedora, starched collar, tie and three-piece suit. DOOLITTLE COLLECTION, AIR FORCE ACADEMY

Jimmy chafed at the many hours marching on the drill field and taking the required ground school courses. He wanted to fly and was afraid the war would be over before he could graduate. He was also concerned that he would lose his girl friend Joe who had finally agreed to marry him. On Christmas Eve, 1917, the two went to the Los Angeles City Hall and were married by a county clerk just before the office closed. Joe paid for the license with money her mother had given her for Christmas.

Jimmy began flight training in January 1918 at Rockwell Field near San Diego and soloed in a Curtiss Jenny after eight hours of instruction. He received the wings of an Army Air Service pilot and a commission as a second lieutenant on March 11, 1918.

Doolittle's desire to get into combat was not to be realized. Instead, he was sent to several fields for training but ended back at Rockwell Field as a flying instructor for advanced students. Although he chafed at first, he decided that if he had to be an instructor, he would be the best they ever had. In order to teach others, he felt compelled to perform every maneuver in the book to perfection. He spent countless extra hours practicing aerobatics and testing his limitations.

It wasn't long before Doolittle was known as a daredevil pilot who would try anything. He teamed up with a brother pilot and the pair would practice wing walking. While one flew, the other would climb out of the cockpit and do handstands on the top wing or skin-the-cat on the axle between the wheels—stunts that were definitely against the rules. One day, Cecil B. DeMille, famous maker of "spectacle" motion pictures, was filming takeoff and landing scenes at the base. As his cameramen were grinding away, he saw a Jenny on the approach with a man calmly sitting on the axle between the wheels. DeMille's cameras followed the plane to its parking spot and recorded the passenger laughing while he and the pilot walked away.

The next day, DeMille showed the scene to Colonel Harvey Burwell, the base commander. "That's Doolittle!" he shouted. He turned to his executive officer and told him to find Doolittle and ground him for a month.

"Joe" and Jimmy documented their engagement in 1916 by posing for this portrait. They were married on Christmas Eve, 1917 while Jimmy was in aviation ground school at the University of California. "Joe" paid for the marriage license. AUTHOR'S COLLECTION

At left, Lt. J.H. Doolittle's official photo after commissioning, March 1918, and at right, a brand new Second Lieutenant poses for a professional photographer.
DOOLITTLE COLLECTION, AIR FORCE ACADEMY

This was only the beginning of Doolittle's flying transgressions. He sought permission to lead a flight of three Curtiss Jennys from San Diego to New York for publicity purposes but two planes were wrecked and Doolittle was ordered to return to San Diego. He landed in a plowed field and the plane was damaged when it turned over but, with help from farmers, he was able to fly it to Rockwell Field.

Doolittle did not get into combat and when the war ended in November 1918, he was transferred to Eagle Pass, Texas to patrol the Mexican border against smugglers, illegal border crossings and raids by bandits. He stayed there about a year and then was transferred to Kelly Field, San Antonio, Texas where he had the opportunity to learn about aircraft engines and structures. It was here he got the idea to attempt a flight across the United States and set a record. Others had tried and only Calbraith P. Rodgers, a civilian, had succeeded in 1911 but it had taken him 49 days to fly from New York to Pasadena and he had crashed 39 times. Doolittle thought he could do it in less than 24 hours.

Before he was permitted to try, he was assigned to Langley Field, Virginia to participate in bombing tests led by Brig. Gen. William "Billy" Mitchell. History was made on July 21, 1921 when the German battleship *Ostfriesland* was sunk by Army bombers. Doolittle flew several bombing missions and developed great respect for Mitchell's theories about air power, although he did not agree with his methods of gaining public attention.

Back in San Antonio, Doolittle received permission to proceed with plans to modify a DH-4 to contain enough fuel so the coast-to-coast flight could be made with only one stop. He flew to Pablo Beach, Florida in May 1922 but crashed on takeoff before a bevy of reporters. Embarrassed, he received permission to try again and took off without any reporters present on the night of September 4, 1922. He encountered thunderstorms en route to Kelly Field but evaded them and landed next morning at 7 a.m. A group of mechanics serviced the plane and he was off an hour later.

Doolittle knew he would be tired toward the end of the trip and had asked for two planes to intercept him at Yuma thinking that the sight of them would help him stay awake. They met him and the trio arrived at San Diego. Doolittle had flown for 21 hours, 19 minutes, the first time anyone had crossed the continent in less than a day. His flight sparked the beginning of many distance and speed record attempts by army aviators to gain public support for military aviation.

The Doolittle family grew during this period. James, Jr. was born in 1920 and John followed in 1922. Jimmy was transferred to McCook Field, Dayton, Ohio, the Army Air Service's major research and testing facility. He attended the Air Service Engineering School there and was thrust into an atmosphere of aeronautical research and testing which gave him the opportunity to

A crowd gathers around Doolittle's DH-4B at Pablo Beach, Florida as he prepares for takeoff on his first attempt to set a transcontinental speed record. The flight ended during the takeoff when the plane's wheels caught in the soft sand; the plane swerved and flipped over in the surf. AUTHOR'S COLLECTION

Doolittle (standing, third from left) poses with personnel at Kelly Field, San Antonio, who helped modify and service the deHavilland DH-4 for his transcontinental flight in 1922. U.S. AIR FORCE PHOTO

Mechanics check over the condition of the DH-4 that had been modified with the addition of a 140-gallon fuel tank and a 24-gallon oil tank in the front seat area. Doolittle was the first to pilot an aircraft from coast-to-coast in less than a day. He later received the Distinguished Flying Cross for this flight. DOOLITTLE COLLECTION

Jimmy, Sr. and Jimmy, Jr. are snapped by a news photographer before Doolittle departs San Antonio for the second half of the transcontinental flight. AUTHOR'S COLLECTION

Doolittle, tired and dirty, but pleased with his progress at the mid-point on the record-setting cross-country flight in September 1922, waits while a maintenance crew at Kelly Field, San Antonio, services his plane. DOOLITTLE COLLECTION, AIR FORCE ACADEMY

participate in actual flight tests and developed in him a keen appreciation of the need for continuing aeronautical research and development.

Doolittle wanted more formal education in engineering. The University of California gave him credit for his last year of college based on his Air Service engineering experience so he applied for entrance to the Massachusetts Institute of Technology to work on a Master of Science degree. He was promptly accepted and in July 1923 moved Joe and the boys to the Boston area for two years of tough but rewarding engineering courses. He wrote his thesis based on acceleration tests he performed on a Fokker PW-7 aircraft at McCook during March 1924 and received his master's degree the following June. He immediately requested to stay at MIT to complete a doctorate and researched the effect of the wind velocity gradient on the flying qualities of an airplane. He made 292 test flights in three different types of aircraft. He received a Doctor of Science degree in 1925 and returned to McCook Field to be made head of the flight test section.

Competition between the army and navy for government funds for aviation was reaching a crescendo during the 1920s. Army and navy pilots competed in air races to attempt to set new speed records and the opportunity came in 1925 to compete for the Pulitzer and Schneider Cup races. The Pulitzer prize for land planes was won at Mitchel Field, New York on October 12, 1925 by Army Lt. Cyrus Bettis flying a Curtiss R3C. To complete for the Schneider Cup, a race for seaplanes, Doolittle practiced flying an R3C on floats at the Navy's Anacostia Field in Washington, D.C. The race was held in October 1925 and Doolittle won it over six other pilots while setting a new record for seaplanes of 232.573 mph. Not satisfied, he took off next day and set still another record of 245.713 mph.

When Jimmy and Joe Doolittle returned to McCook Field, they were given a memorable reception. They were invited to a dinner in downtown Dayton and fellow test pilots persuaded Jimmy to put on an admiral's uniform and sit in a lifeboat mounted on a truck while it was pulled in a parade around the city. On each side of the boat were signs that read: "Admiral James H. Doolittle?"

Although the new speed record was widely publicized, it was not until August 1929 that

Doolittle enrolled at the Massachusetts Institute of Technology in 1924 to pursue the courses for master's and doctoral degrees in engineering. "Joe" Doolittle, rented a special typewriter and typed his thesis and dissertation. He was the only active duty military pilot to hold an earned doctorate for many years. DOOLITTLE COLLECTION, AIR FORCE ACADEMY

Doolittle was awarded the Mackay Trophy for winning the race four years before. Clarence H. Mackay had established the trophy in 1912 for competitions for military aviators. If there were no annual contest, the War Department could award it to those who had made the most meritorious flight of the year. The delay in awarding it to Doolittle was never explained.

Now famous as a racing pilot, the Curtiss airplane firm asked to "borrow" Doolittle to demonstrate their new P-1 Hawk fighter plane in South America. Permission was granted and he sailed to Chile in 1926. There were pilot/salesmen there from German, French, Italian and British firms and the Chileans wanted them to compete against each other for their order. Doolittle was delighted to be invited to match his skill and judgment against others in the air.

A cocktail party was held in an officer's club for the foreign pilots and Jimmy was introduced to a potent drink called a pisco sour. During the evening, the subject of Douglas Fairbanks came

Doolittle had never flown a seaplane until he practiced in this Curtiss R3C-2 racer for the Schneider Cup Race in October 1925. The race was held off Bay Shore Park near Baltimore, Md. Doolittle placed first with a speed of 232.573 mph. He later received the Mackay Trophy for winning the race. Immediately afterward, he made a record-setting speed of 245.713 mph. AUTHOR'S COLLECTION

General Mason M. Patrick (right), Chief of Army Air Service, was present to congratulate Doolittle for his Schneider Cup victory. "Joe" Doolittle was also there for the race. U.S. AIR FORCE PHOTO

After receiving the Schneider Cup for winning the 1925 seaplane race, Doolittle's friends mounted a lifeboat on a truck and against his will paraded him through Dayton dressed as a navy admiral to celebrate his victory over the navy's best racing pilots. U.S. AIR FORCE PHOTO

up. Fairbanks was a famous American acrobatic movie actor noted for his balcony-leaping, sword-wielding heroic scenes that had captured the imaginations of Latin Americans. Doolittle playfully bragged that all Americans could do those things and even he could do them. The guests wanted him to prove it.

Doolittle went into a handstand and then walked across the lounge on his hands. There was polite clapping but it wasn't enough. He moved over to a window leading to a balcony and went into a handstand on the ledge. There was more clapping but Doolittle wasn't through yet. He grasped the ledge with one hand, extended his body straight out parallel with the ground, a feat requiring strong arms and a knowledge of body leverage.

There were shouts of "Bravo!" and "Ole!" but Doolittle felt something happening. The ledge began to crumble and he plunged to the courtyard below. He was rushed to the hospital and x-rays showed that he had broken both ankles which were immediately put in casts. It seemed now that his air demonstrations in Chile were over and the Chileans would not have the benefit of seeing an American plane perform. He was advised to remain in the hospital for several weeks and wear casts for about two months.

Embarrassed and furious at himself, Doolittle would have none of this. He asked Boyd Sherman, his mechanic, to make clips for the Hawk's rudder pedals. Two days later, Doolittle was helped into the cockpit and ready to fly while Karl A. von Schoenebeck, an arrogant World War I German ace, was putting a Dornier through a solo aerobatic routine that caused the crowd to applaud frequently. Doolittle' competitive blood boiled and the crowd watched as he was helped into the Hawk's cockpit. He took off, climbed to altitude, made a fast pass at the Dornier and the dogfight was on. Von Schoenebeck zoomed after the Curtiss only to find that the Dornier was badly outclassed. Doolittle whipped the sensitive P-1 into reverse turns and fast climbs and dives so quickly that the Dornier seemed clumsy by comparison.

The German pilot suddenly broke off the engagement and headed for the airport. As he followed, Doolittle saw that a huge piece of fabric had torn loose from the Dornier's upper wing, certainly not a good omen for a plane that was supposed to survive the rigors of combat maneuvers. As von Schoenebeck landed, Doolittle made a victory pass over the field, inverted. Never before had the Chileans seen such flying. The American had beaten the German with his feet

Doolittle was placed on extended leave from the army without pay in 1926 to demonstrate the Curtiss P-1 Hawk fighter plane in South America. He broke both ankles while performing acrobatics at a cocktail party in Santiago, Chile. His ankles were put in casts and he continued demonstration flights in Bolivia, Brazil and Argentina. He is shown here with William H. McMullen (l), Curtiss pilot, and Jerry Van Wagoner, mechanic. DOOLITTLE COLLECTION

in casts!

It had not been easy for Doolittle. Those extreme maneuvers put painful pressure on his ankles and he almost passed out when he taxied in and shut the engine down. But he quickly revived when he heard the cheers and applause from the spectators.

The casts on both legs had been strained and cracked but the doctor refused to have anything to do with the crazy Yankee. Doolittle asked Boyd Sherman to find an artificial limb maker to make him two strong, reinforced casts. Sherman devised new clips for the rudder pedals and tightened them after Doolittle was seated in the cockpit. Doolittle then flew to La Paz, Bolivia for more demonstrations and then over the Andes Mountains to Argentina. He thus became the first American to fly across the Andes but few knew how risky it was for Doolittle. Not only was he flying a single-engine aircraft with both legs in casts and fitted into the rudder clips but he did not have a parachute since he could not get his feet unstrapped from the clips if he had to bail out.

He demonstrated the perky fighter plane for the Argentinians who bought the P-1 for their air force. He returned home by boat with his legs still in casts and spent the rest of the summer of 1926 in Walter Reed Hospital in Washington so that his mangled ankles could heal properly.

Four Doolittles Unhurt in Plane Wreck Aground

Stunt Flyer, Wife, Children Roll From Ship Capsized by Mitchel Field Wind

Special to the Herald Tribune

MITCHEL FIELD, L.I., Feb. 16. - A gust of wind that upset his cream-colored Lockheed-Vega monoplane on the field almost ended the career of former Lieutenant James H. Doolittle, once holder of the world's airplane speed record and the stunting ace of the Army air forces, as he was preparing to leave here today with Mrs. Doolittle and their two children to enter his first position as a civilian pilot. All four scrambled unhurt from the wreckage of the machine, which was badly damaged.

Lieutenant Doolittle's resignation from the Army took effect on February 1. He has been appointed head of the aeronautical department of the Shell Oil Company in St. Louis, and his flight today, bound for his new home, was to have been his farewell to his friends at Mitchel Field.

Children Eager for Ride

The household goods of the Doolittle family have been shipped to St. Louis, and the children, James Jr., eight years old, and John, six, have been looking forward with excited anticipation to today's journey. Lieutenant Doolittle preferred to fly rather than travel by rail.

"Trains aren't safe," he said. Nevertheless, he and his family left the Pennsylvania station on a train for the West because he couldn't wait for his plane to be repaired.

Hundreds of Lieutenant Doolittle's friends, pilots and mechanics from Mitchel and Roosevelt Fields, and persons from New York, swarmed about his ship at 12:30 p.m. as he supervised the packing of the hand baggage and arranged Mrs. Doolittle and the children comfortably in the cockpit. When all was snug Doolittle waved his hand and the roar of his motor drowned a chorus of farewells.

Machine Is Capsized

A thirty-mile wind, gusty and cold, was sweeping the field as the machine taxied down toward the far corner. Observers noticed that Doolittle was having trouble keeping a straight course. Just before he reached the corner he started to turn in order to head into the wind before leaving the ground.

A sharper thrust of wind cut in suddenly from a new quarter. The craft wavered sickeningly an instant and then dipped over on its left side, scraping along the ground for several yards before it halted.

There was a moment of anxious excitement as the crowd broke into a run toward the wreck. The foremost reached it in time to see the lieutenant and Mrs. Doolittle brushing off the clothes of the two boys, who gazed in surprise at the worried faces of the bystanders.

"Well, dad," said James Jr., I guess we won't get off today after all."

Not one of the four passengers in the ship even was scratched. But an inspection of the plane revealed considerable damage.

The propeller was bent almost double, the left wing was crumpled up and a wing gasoline tank cracked, the landing gear was wrecked and part of the fuselage stove in. Doolittle salvaged his baggage and trudged back across the field to the pilots' quarters.

Late in the afternoon the party left by automobile for New York, ready to board a train for their destination. The wrecked airplane was taken to the plant of the Air Associates, Inc., at Roosevelt Field, where it will be repaired.

Lieutenant Doolittle's record as a pilot has been sensational. Today's crash was his third in a year without injury. Last March he tipped over in landing at an emergency field aat Kenilworth, N.J. But his most spectacular escape came at the national air races at Cleveland last September 1.

Lieutenant Doolittle was practicing about five miles out of town, over open country, for a series of difficult stunts which he was planning to exhibit at the air carnival later in the afternoon. Suddenly the wings of his Curtiss pursuit plane folded up. The lieutenant stepped from the cockpit 2,000 feet up and drifted to the ground in his parachute.

A motorist brought him into Cleveland and he walked unconcernedly into the airport just as the nation's leading aviators were beginning to worry about him.

"I'm afraid I'll have to have another ship," he said. His only injury was a pin scratch on his hand and a wounded tongue which he had bitten and then forgot until hours later. He performed the same stunts that had caused his crash a short time before. Thousands of spectators knew nothing of his narrow escape until that evening.

A few weeks later Lieutenant Doolittle startled the flying world again. Sitting in a cockpit so covered by canvas that he could see nothing outside, he took off from Mitchel Field, flew for fifteen minutes and made a perfect landing with nothing but his sight of his instrument board to guide him. This feat was the final step in the plan of the Guggenheim Fund to evolve a method of flying in foggy weather, when all vision is blotted out.

Lieutenant Doolittle was attached to the 1st Pursuit Group at Selfridge Field, Mount Clemens, Mich., when he was sent on detached duty to Mitchel Field to test airplanes for the Guggenheim safe aircraft competition. Later, he was active in the Guggenheim research in fog-flying conditions.

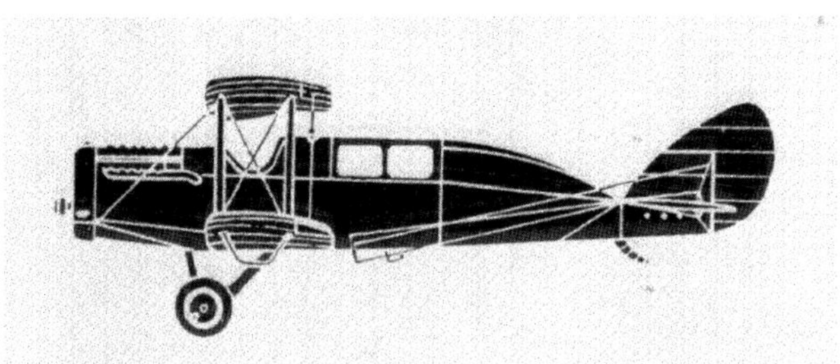

Chapter 4
The Most Significant Contribution to Aviation

The army doctors gave Doolittle an order: remain inactive for six months to let the badly damaged ankles heal. To a vigorous man like Doolittle, it was a difficult "sentence" to accept. However, his mind remained active and it gave him a chance to think about what he could do when he returned to the cockpit. He considered new aerobatic stunts that had never been attempted; one of them was the outside loop, a maneuver that all pilots thought impossible.

The normal, or inside, loop is a relatively easy maneuver in any aircraft. Nose the plane down to gather speed, then pull firmly on the elevator control until the plane is inverted, then continue back pressure on the stick and around into level flight. In an outside loop, the pilot would be on the outside of the circle and tremendous gravity forces would be acting on his body as well as on the plane. But there was a basic question: If a plane was strong enough to withstand such a strain, could a pilot's body withstand the centrifugal force that would tend to burst his blood vessels and force his organs toward his throat?

Doolittle carefully analyzed the stresses that would be placed on an aircraft and concluded that the average American fighter plane, stressed to seven times gravity, could take the strain. He asked the doctors at the hospital what effect such a maneuver would have on a man and no one knew. Even if a plane did not have a structural failure, some thought that the centrifugal pressure would cause the pilot to suffer a brain hemorrhage. At the very least, he would "black out" and lose control of the plane.

The question became an obsession with Doolittle. Anxious to get back into test flying at McCook Field when he was released from the hospital, he began a series of maneuvers in the Curtiss P-1 Hawk which would lead to an eventual try at an outside loop.

To find out how much pressure he could stand, Doolittle flew inverted for extended periods and then practiced pushing the nose up into a climb until the speed was gone and the plane stalled. He analyzed his own physical reactions and checked the plane over thoroughly after each flight for any wing failure. On May 25, 1927, confident that he and the Curtiss Hawk could both take the strain, he told a few of his fellow pilots what he planned to do. Word spread quickly and pilots and mechanics watched as he climbed to 10,000 feet. He pushed the nose over until the plane was upside down. He continued the forward pressure before he became nearly unconscious. Just as he thought he might fail, the plane nosed upward and swung over the top into level flight. He had successfully completed an outside loop, the first pilot in history to do so and had witnesses to prove it.

As soon as he heard about the flight, Major General Mason M. Patrick, Chief of the Army Air Corps, prohibited Army pilots from performing outside loops because most military aircraft were not stressed for such a maneuver and he considered them dangerous for both plane and pilot. From then on during air shows, Doolittle continued to do a half outside loop with a half roll at the bottom to level flight.

What was important to Doolittle was that he had proved that the development of military aircraft had reached a point where the pilot could rely on the strength of his plane to perform such a high stress maneuver. His success was widely publicized and his public image became that of a devil-may-care pilot who would try anything in an airplane at least once. What was not known was that he had approached the question scientifically, assessed the facts and theorized what the outcome would be. He combined the traits of the daredevil with those of an aeronautical engineer. It was a calculated risk and he was a master at it.

Jimmy was invited by Curtiss to visit South America again on leave from the Army in 1928, this time to demonstrate the P-1 and an O-1, a new observation plane. The O-1 was wrecked by

Returning to South America in June 1928 for a second Curtiss demonstration tour, Doolittle put the P-1 Hawk and an O-2 observation plane through extensive maneuvers to prove their versatility. The P-1 was put on floats and Doolittle is shown at the Argentine Naval Seaplane Base at Puerto Belgrano adjusting the hook to lift the plane to the dock for display. DOOLITTLE COLLECTION, AIR FORCE ACADEMY

a British pilot in Peru, leaving only the P-1 to be demonstrated. He decided to finish the tour by setting speed records between cities. He flew from Santiago, Chile to Buenos Aires, Argentina in six hours, beating his own previous record by a half hour. From there he flew to Asuncion, Paraguay to set a record between the two capitals, then made the first flight ever attempted over the Mato Grosso, Brazil's impenetrable jungle.

The American ambassadors in each country were delighted with the image Doolittle portrayed with the Latin Americans and sent many favorable reports to Washington. It was said this one-man goodwill tour had done more for a favorable impression of the United States in just six months than visits by U. S. Navy ships and various diplomatic gestures had done in the previous decade.

Doolittle returned to his assignment at McCook Field and wondered what the future held for him. The answer came in an invitation to participate in experiments to be conducted by the Daniel Guggenheim Fund for the Promotion of Aeronautics. The Fund was established by philanthropist Guggenheim in January 1926 "to promote the advance of the art, science and business of aviation" One phase of the Fund's work was to study the means of assuring safe and reliable flight despite weather conditions, including the dissipation of fog and development of cockpit instruments that would allow airplanes to fly safely in fog and other low visibility situations.

A Full Flight Laboratory was established at Mitchel Field, New York and Doolittle was borrowed from the Air Corps to make the flight tests. He, Joe and their two lively boys, moved into barracks at Mitchel Field, N.Y. in the fall of 1928. Two planes were bought for experimental flying: a Vought O2U-1 Corsair for cross-country practice and an Army NY-2 trainer which had been fitted with enlarged Navy trainer wings. The latter was to be used as a flying laboratory for instrument landing experiments and to test instruments, equipment or devices that might be helpful in overcoming fog problems. Professor William G. Brown of MIT monitored the tests and Lt.

EVENING NEWS, FRIDAY, MARCH 15, 1929

Flier Crashes In Fog Test

Army Expert Out of Gas at Kenilworth After Circling Newark

Flying by instruments in a dense fog last night, Lieutenant James H. Doolittle, crack army pilot who has been conducting fog flying tests for the Guggenheim Fund for Promotion of Aeronautics, wrecked his plane when he made a forced landing at Kenilworth. The flier was shaken and bruised but otherwise uninjured.

Lieutenant Doolittle was forced down when his gasoline was almost exhausted as he circled Northern New Jersey looking for Mitchel Field, Long

Lieutenant James H. Doolittle.

Island. He was flying his speedy Vought Corsair from Buffalo to Mitchel Field when he became lost in the dense fog over the Hudson.

Flying low to pick up landmarks, his plane missed striking the buttresses of the new bridge at Fort Lee by only a few feet. He climbed out of danger, but could not determine his position from lights and dropped low again. This time he narrowly missed hitting the mast of a steamer.

Gets Bearings Here.

Circling over Nothern New Jersey, Lieutenant Doolittle was unable to find Teterboro Field and finally came over Newark. The roar of his 410-horse-power Wasp engine was heard at Newark Airport and Thomas J. Donnelly, night manager, switched on the flood-lights.

The army flier evidently wanted to get to Mitchel Field, however, and did not land. He circled the field, which he is familiar with, and then, thinking he was heading toward Mitchel Field, flew over Newark. The Vought Corsair circled the electric sign of The Newark Evening News twice, but Lieutenant Doolittle again lost his way and headed south.

When his gasoline supply became low he realized he would have to land within a few minutes. The beacon light for air mail fliers at Kenilworth attracted him and he headed toward it. His gasoline was exhausted and his engine stopped during the glide.

Flier Unhurt, Gear, Smashed.

Lieutenant Doolittle circled low over a small patch of open ground but as he prepared to land a group of trees loomed directly ahead. He jumped the ship over the short trees and set it down near Faitoute avenue, Kenilworth. It ran along the ground and crashed into a scrub oak, turning over.

Both wings and the landing gear were smashed but the flier was unhurt. Paul H. VanDerZee, who lives nearby, ran to the plane and found Lieutenant Doolittle climbing into the upturned cockpit to get his baggage. VanDerZee told the Army flier that he and several friends had tried with flashlights to attract the plane to the field of the Union County Flying Club, a short distance from the beacon.

Lieutenant Doolittle left his baggage at the home of John Arthur in New Orange Park, Kenilworth, a half mile from the spot where he landed. He refused medical treatment and went to New York by train. He will send a truck today to get the plane.

Plane Heard Here.

The exhaust of Lieutenant Doolittle's plane was heard plainly over Newark, Elizabeth and nearby towns and many persons telephoned Newark Airport, thinking it was a mail plane. Reports from every section were that the plane was within 150 feet of the ground.

Lieutenant Doolittle was the first flier to make an outside loop, the most difficult flying maneuver. Airport officials said he undoubtedly could have landed with safety at Newark Airport but used the field only to fix his position. He is well known at the airport, having visited the field several times.

Newark Evening News article from Friday, March 15, 1929, which told the story of Lieutenant Doolittle's foggy crash. Luckily, Doolittle was not seriously injured.

Mitchel Field, New York in the 1920s.

Doolittle was "loaned" by the Army in 1928-29 to head the Full Flight Laboratory sponsored by the Guggenheim Fund for the Promotion of Aeronautics at Mitchel Field, New York. The Vought O2U Corsair shown here was used during the tests for cross-country flights. U.S. AIR FORCE PHOTO

Benjamin S. Kelsey was assigned to assist as a safety pilot, with Sgt. Jack Dalton as mechanic. Harry Guggenheim, son of Daniel, also assisted, along with Capt. Emory S. Land, a naval officer.

As preliminary practice flights progressed, it was apparent that the instruments then in use were not adequate. The magnetic compass, due to the northerly turning error, was entirely unsatisfactory for determining a precise heading when maneuvering or landing. The turn-and-bank indicator was more a qualitative than a quantitative instrument. More reliable, easy-to-read instruments were needed to show an exact heading and more precise altitude, especially for the initial and final stages of blind landings.

Doolittle sketched out a rough diagram of the dial for an instrument he thought would do the job and showed it to Elmer Sperry, Sr., an inventor who headed the Sperry Gyroscope Co. Sperry recommended two instruments instead: an artificial horizon and a directional gyroscope. Doolittle made a number of flights testing these instruments with Elmer Sperry, Jr. who had been assigned to work on the project. He also worked with Paul Kollsman, a young German emigre who had set up a shop in a Brooklyn garage to develop a barometric altimeter that was more precise and responded to changes in altitude without lagging. These basic instruments with their much improved descendants are standard on most aircraft today.

It was during the radio phase of testing that a visual cockpit indicator was needed for the precise direction control needed during the final phase of blind landings. As tests progressed, the instrumentation improved and considerable thought was given to the arrangement of the instruments to facilitate reading them and to reduce pilot fatigue. Doolittle made over 200 blind landings with the cockpit completely covered by a hood and Kelsey as the safety pilot. He felt he was ready by September 1929 to make an actual blind flight.

Heavy fog covered Mitchel Field on the morning of September 24, 1929 but no flying had been planned; instead, an experiment would be con-

Doolittle poses beside the Consolidated NY-2 trainer that was used throughout the blind flying experiments at Mitchel Field, NY in 1929. Lt. Ben Kelsey flew as the safety pilot in the front cockpit; the rear cockpit was completely covered during the tests. U.S. AIR FORCE PHOTO

With the safety pilot in the front seat, Doolittle placed a hood over the rear cockpit and made numerous practice flights. He made one unofficial solo flight in the fog on September 24, 1929 before making a flight with witnesses present the same day. U.S. AIR FORCE PHOTO

The instrument panel in the NY-2 varied many times during the blind flight experiments to ascertain the best grouping for the pilot. The Kollsman sensitive altimeter in this display was mounted on a block of wood above and to the right of the panel. The special radio beacon direction finder control is the octagon-shaped device in the lower left hand corner. The Sperry artificial horizon is the left -most dial in the bottom row. U.S. AIR FORCE PHOTO

An intense Doolittle waits to start another instrument test flight. Note the hood that he will pull over his cockpit to ensure that he cannot see outside. The safety pilot occupied the front cockpit to watch out for other aircraft and take the controls if necessary. U.S. AIR FORCE PHOTO

ducted to try to burn off the fog with a giant blow torch apparatus but it was unsuccessful. "We were disappointed," Doolittle recalled. "We were there and the fog was there, so I decided to make a real fog flight."

The NY-2 was warmed up and the ground radios turned on. Doolittle taxied out alone to the middle of the field, took off and climbed up through the fog. He turned and flew until he was in an approach position to the field and dropped through the fog to a landing without seeing any reference outside the plane. Mr. Guggenheim was told what Doolittle had done and was asked to come to the field to witness an "official" blind flight and landing. Although the fog had burned off by the time he arrived, Doolittle wanted to make the flight alone under the hood but Guggenheim insisted that Lt. Ben Kelsey occupy the front seat to take over if necessary because there was other air traffic in the vicinity.

The hood was closed and Kelsey lined the plane up for takeoff. Kelsey, in the front open cockpit, conspicuously held his hands over his head as proof that Doolittle was flying blind. Doolittle took off under the hood, climbed to 1,000 feet, leveled off and made a 180-degree turn to the left. He flew for several miles, turned to intercept the Mitchel Field range and started the NY-2 on a gradual descent. He leveled off at 200 feet and flew until he passed the radio fan marker on the east side of the field. He then flew the plane down to the ground from that point, using the blind landing procedure he had developed. Kelsey kept his hands resting on top of the wing where they could be seen and never had to take over the controls. The flight took only 15 minutes but it was the first time in history that witnesses were present to affirm that an airplane had made a take-off, flew a set course, and landed by the use of instruments alone.

Those short flights that early September morning marked the entrance of American aviation into a new phase of development. While it did not represent the final solution to the problem of flying through weather conditions and night operations that had previously grounded planes and prevented scheduled operations, it did lay the essential ground work for the blind flying techniques used today. Much more work remained for commercial and government organizations to prepare facilities, manufacture radio equipment, and train pilots before an optimistic headline in the *New York Times* – FOG PERIL OVERCOME — could be realized.

The Fund was disbanded and other pilots at McCook Field took over where Doolittle's work left off. Lt. Albert F. Hegenberger made the first *official* solo blind flight on May 9, 1932. Flying by instruments soon outgrew the early experimental phase and became a practical reality. Doolittle

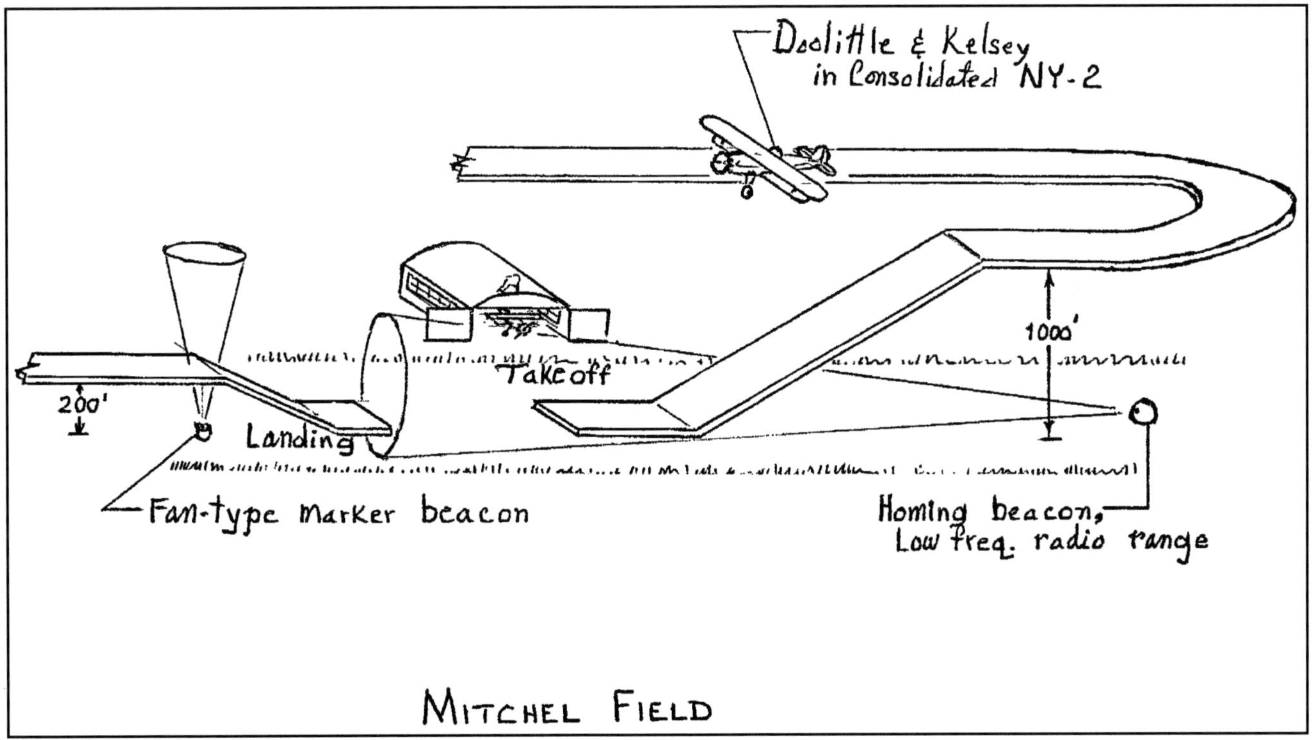

Four of the men responsible for the success of the first blind flight in history reunite at Boonton, New Jersey in September 1979 during the 50th anniversary of that flight. They are (l to r) Paul Kollsman, inventor of the sensitive altimeter, Doolittle, Dr. Lewis M. Hull, former president Aircraft Radio & Control Co., and Brig. Gen. Benjamin S. Kelsey, safety pilot and later head of the Air Force All-Weather Flying Division. PHOTO BY THE AUTHOR

was grateful for the opportunity to participate in those initial experiments. It was his most significant contribution to aviation.

That night of September 24, 1929 was party time for those who had been associated with the blind flying experimentation. All who participated autographed Joe Doolittle's large white damask tablecloth. Afterward, Joe embroidered the signatures in black thread to preserve them. Over the years, she painstakingly stitched over 500 signatures of famous visitors and friends on the tablecloth, then more on napkins when she ran out of space. The tablecloth was later donated to the National Air & Space Museum.

The work at Mitchel Field did not occupy all of Doolittle's time during 1929. He was asked to put on an aerobatic demonstration at the 1929 Cleveland Air Races and borrowed a P-1 from the Ohio National Guard. As usual, he took off to practice his repertoire before stunting before the crowd. Remembering that General Patrick had ordered that Air Corps pilots should not perform outside loops, he took off, climbed to 4,000 feet to do the first half of one, and began a dive. When he was about 30 degrees past the vertical at about 2,000 feet, there was a sharp pop and the wings began to peel back from the fuselage. The Hawk slowed down and began to tumble. Doolittle unbuckled his safety belt and was thrown out of the cockpit. When he was clear of the plane, he jerked the parachute rip cord and the 'chute came open at about 1,000 feet. He landed safely in a field at Olmsted Falls near Cleveland and was driven back to the air races. He borrowed another P-1 and put on his half outside loop as a finale to the program. Afterward, he wrote to the Irwin Parachute Co. and thanked the workers with a note saying, "Airplane failed. Parachute worked." He was promptly made a member of the Caterpillar Club, an exclusive group whose members have jumped out of an aircraft and used a parachute to save their lives.

Doolittle was required to fill out an official report of the P-1 crash and his bailout. Under the question, "Cause for the emergency jump," he stated: "Wings broke." To describe his method of leaving the aircraft, he wrote: "Thrown out."

Shortly afterward, Doolittle received a letter from the Army's adjutant general stating that he had been awarded the Distinguished Flying Cross twice for his 1922 cross-country flight and in recognition of acceleration tests he had made during March 1924 at McCook Field. The DFC had been authorized by a 1926 act of Congress.

In January 1930, he received another surprise. He had been selected to receive the Harmon Trophy, Ligue des Aviateurs for his instrument work with the Guggenheim Fund the year before.

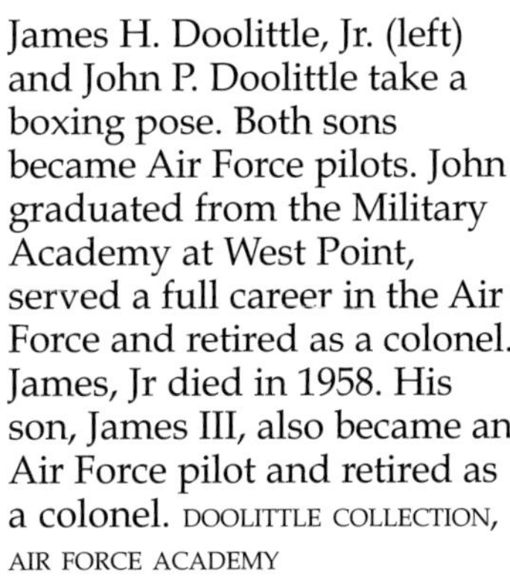

The evening of Doolittle's first successful blind flying flight in 1929, a number of guests signed Mrs. Doolittle's tablecloth in pencil. Afterward, any guest who had a meal at their house was invited to do the same. When "Joe" accompanied her husband on trips, she carefully embroidered the signatures in black silk. The signings include famous personalities in aviation, business and entertainment. The tablecloth was donated to the National Air & Space Museum. DOOLITTLE COLLECTION

James H. Doolittle, Jr. (left) and John P. Doolittle take a boxing pose. Both sons became Air Force pilots. John graduated from the Military Academy at West Point, served a full career in the Air Force and retired as a colonel. James, Jr died in 1958. His son, James III, also became an Air Force pilot and retired as a colonel. DOOLITTLE COLLECTION, AIR FORCE ACADEMY

YORK

Tribune

LATE CITY EDITION

MBER 5, 1931 * * * * TWO CENTS In Greater New York | THREE CENTS Within 200 Miles | FOUR CENTS Elsewhere

Ending Record Flight From Coast

Doolittle Flies Across Nation In 11¼ Hrs. to Break Record

Ex-Army Major Halts at Cleveland to Win Race and $7,500, Continues to Newark for $2,500

Averages 218 M.P.H., California to Jersey

Harold S. Johnson Is Second, Crusader Last, as 2 of 8 Fail to Finish; President Hails Air Progress

By Francis Walton
A Staff Correspondent

CLEVELAND, Sept. 4.—Major James H. Doolittle, formerly of the Army Air Corps, flew from Los Angeles to New York (Newark Airport) in 11 hours 15 minutes today, setting a transcontinental air record and also winning the Bendix trophy race of the National Air Races when he landed his plane here shortly after 3 o'clock this afternoon.

He won $7,500 for this achievement and continued to Newark, N. J., to break the 12 hours 25 minutes 3 seconds mark established by Captain Frank M. Hawks on August 13, 1930, to win an additional purse of $2,500. He remained at Newark only long enough to refuel and then sped back over the Allegheny Mountains in his Wasp-powered Laird racer, landing here at 7:45 o'clock, New York daylight time, tonight.

Plane Overhauled

He trundled his special racing plane, the Cleveland Speed Foundation entry, which he will pilot in the Thompson Trophy race, into a hangar for engine change and overhaul. After seeing this work started, Major Doolittle left as a passenger in a two-seated plane, piloted by James Haizlip, of Chicago, for St. Louis, on a business trip. He said he would be back here tomorrow morning to test his plane over the Thompson Trophy course. He arrived in St. Louis late this evening.

Major Doolittle's flying today once across the continent and part of the way back ranks as one of the great achievements in human travel. He flew

IN REPLY REFER TO
FILE

DEPARTMENT OF COMMERCE
AERONAUTICS BRANCH
WASHINGTON

VIOLATION FILE

NOTICE OF VIOLATION
OF AIR COMMERCE REGULATIONS
BY OWNER OR PERSON IN COMMAND OF AIRCRAFT INVOLVING
INCURRENCE OF PENALTY
(Air Commerce Act of 1926)

To: James H. Doolittle,
c/o Shell Oil Company,
St. Louis, Mo.

You are hereby notified that you are subject to a civil penalty of Five Hundred Dollars ($500.00) for violation of the Air Traffic Rules at Kansas City, Missouri, on October 1, 1930. You are charged with the following violations, each of which constitutes a separate and distinct offense:

Acrobatically flying aircraft over an established airport;
Performing acrobatics at a height less than 1,500 feet.

If there are any mitigating circumstances upon which you propose to premise a request for mitigation or remission of the imposition of the civil penalty of Five Hundred Dollars ($500.00), it is in order for you to transmit to the Secretary of Commerce a detailed sworn statement, in duplicate, within fifteen (15) days of the date of the receipt of this notification.

Gilbert G. Budwig
Gilbert G. Budwig,
Director of Air Regulation.

Dated October 8, 1930
At Washington, D. C.

Doolittle admitted he was a "mischief maker" in an airplane and was chastised several times during his early stunting days. In this instance, he was able to persuade the Secretary of Commerce to revoke the fine.

Chapter 5

The Second Bailout

The end of the blind flying experiments in 1929 marked a major decision point in the life of Jimmy Doolittle. In spite of his accomplishments and his advanced education, he was still a first lieutenant and had been one since July 1, 1920. Promotions were so slow in peacetime then that he had no idea if he would ever be promoted to captain.

The fame that had come to Doolittle had brought him job offers in private industry. With a wife and two sons to care for, a first lieutenant's pay, which included flying pay, amounted to about $200 a month. Jimmy was grateful for the opportunities that had come his way but he felt he had more to offer the science of aviation. He made his decision in December 1929 when Shell Oil Co. made him an offer to head the aviation division of the company in St. Louis. He resigned his regular commission on February 15, 1930 and asked to be commissioned in the Air Corps Reserve. His request was granted and, to his surprise, he was commissioned a major, skipping the rank of captain.

Part of the arrangement with Shell was that the company would purchase a Lockheed Vega, a fast, barrel-shaped plane that would hold four people and cruise at better than 200 miles an hour. He flew it from the factory in California and intended to fly Joe and the boys from Mitchel Field to St. Louis the day after he was released from the army. He bundled Joe, the boys and their heavy belongings into the trim white Vega and taxied out for takeoff through blowing snow to the runway area. He started the takeoff run but ran into snowdrifts that slowed the plane down. There was a sudden wrenching sound as one of the wheels buckled and the Vega plowed into a snow bank. No one was hurt but the door had jammed and a rescue crew had to get them out.

The plane's wing was smashed and the gas tank was punctured. It would be days before the damage could be repaired. Doolittle was mad at himself and embarrassed. Newspapermen had been watching and reported the incident. He and the family had to take the train to St. Louis, a fate that added to his humiliation. It was a poor way to begin a new job.

The company did not agree and immediately acceded to a request from the Curtiss-Wright Corporation to lend Doolittle and two additional pilots for a four-month tour of Europe to demonstrate four different types of their planes—pursuit, training, reconnaissance and observation. In April 1930, he began the tour with other pilots in Greece, the first of 21 countries. His job was to put on demonstration flights with the Hawk fighter that the Europeans would not forget. He put the aircraft through a series of aerobatics that amazed the crowds wherever the group went.

The trip was more than just flying for Doolittle. He met many military airmen and was shown the latest aeronautical developments in

Lieut. Doolittle Plans Record

Speed Flight From Coast to Coast Contemplated for Spring.

LIEUT. JAMES H. DOOLITTLE, former Wright Field flyer and crack stunt flyer of the United States Army Air Corps, who recently joined the forces of the Shell Oil Company, is reported to have in mind an attempt to establish a new coast-to-coast speed record during the coming Summer, according to word received in his old stamping grounds at Dayton, Ohio. It is understood the oil company will finance the venture.

The record is now held by Capt. Frank Hawks and it was set last year. Hawks now flies for the Texaco Oil Company.

Doolittle, after leaving Wright Field some months ago, was stationed at Mitchel Field, having been loaned to the Guggenheim Foundation to do experimental work.

Sky News, February 13, 1930

Doolittle (in civilian hat) acted as a salesman for Shell Oil and Curtiss-Wright and demonstrated aircraft in 21 European and Middle Eastern countries in 1930. The pilot in helmet and goggles is Capt. (later General) John K. "Joe" Cannon loaned by Curtiss-Wright for the trip. DOOLITTLE COLLECTION, AIR FORCE ACADEMY

the countries he visited. He was particularly concerned about Germany when he saw the emphasis was being placed on fast aircraft which could be the forerunner to developing military aircraft which they were forbidden to do according to the Treaty of Versailles signed after the surrender of Germany after World War I.

Because of what he saw, Doolittle decided to devote the next three years to racing because he knew that racing planes, just as racing automobiles, leads to continual improvements in engines, fuels, lubricants, and safety, as well as speed. He knew his job was to sell the company's products and he could help by flying some of the fastest planes available for racing and testing.

But Doolittle didn't want the company to take an unreasonable financial risk. He took the family savings and bought a Shell-owned Beech Travelair low-wing monoplane that had been wrecked to conduct his own experimentation which the press immediately dubbed the "Mystery Ship." He ordered a new engine and modifications of his own design to streamline the fuselage and change the ailerons which he hoped would make it the world's fastest plane. When it was ready for testing on June 21, 1931, Doolittle taxied out and took off. After testing the plane at altitude, he made a speed run over the airport and was pleased to see the airspeed indicator creep up to 300 miles per hour. He pulled up sharply and heard a heart-stopping, wrenching noise. The plane began to vibrate and seemed about to break apart. He cut the throttle as the wings began to wrench away from the fuselage.

There was only one thing he could do: jump. He pulled himself out of the seat and saw the wings rip off. Using all his strength, he rolled himself over the side of the cockpit and grabbed the ring of his parachute. The slipstream of the wildly gyrating fuselage enabled the parachute to snap open immediately and his feet hit the ground a few seconds later. It was a very close call; he had made one of the lowest successful jumps in history to become a member of the Caterpillar Club for the second time. He was glad that the company had not bought the plane and the financial

Doolittle parachutes from a Curtiss Hawk after its wings tore off while practicing aerobatics at East St. Louis, Illinois in June 1931. Doolittle was not injured and promptly flew another aircraft for an aerobatic demonstration. It was the second of three parachute jumps made during his lifetime of flying. DOOLITTLE COLLECTION, AIR FORCE ACADEMY

risk had been his own.

What bothered Doolittle most, aside from almost losing his life, was that his drawing board calculations had not been good enough. An airplane still had to be flown to see if it could withstand the stresses in flight that were intended. He hoped the aeronautical sciences would eventually prove that wasn't necessary.

Doolittle still wanted to race and contacted E. M. "Matty" Laird, a maker of racing planes. He had produced one that he labeled the Laird *Super Solution,* a biplane powered by a 550-hp Wright Wasp engine and Doolittle borrowed it to enter the 1931 Bendix cross-country race between Burbank, California and Cleveland, Ohio.

Just after midnight on September 4, 1931, eight pilots took off each on their own itineraries and raced the clock. Reports showed the *Super Solution* was leading. After stops at Albuquerque and Kansas City where Shell refueling teams had him on his way quickly, he landed at Cleveland in a light, drizzling rain. His time was 9 hours, 10 minutes, better by four minutes than the next pilot, who was flying a Lockheed *Orion.*

But Doolittle was not satisfied at just winning the Bendix. As the crowd looked on, he helped the gas crew service his plane quickly and took off. He wanted to beat the coast-to-coast record of 12 hours, 25 minutes that Frank Hawks had set the year before. If he could, the Bendix Trophy people said they would add an extra $2,500 to the $7,500 he would receive for winning the race.

Refusing the sandwich that Joe Doolittle offered him, he took off and headed for Newark, New Jersey, knowing that there was a squall line of thunderstorms over the Allegheny Mountains. Fighting fatigue and the weather, the determined Doolittle bored through the rain and lightning and touched down at the Newark Airport 11 hours, 16 minutes after leaving Burbank. He was the first pilot to span the continent in less than half a day, just as exactly nine years before, he had been the first to span the country in less than a day.

Crowds had gathered at the Newark Airport after hearing that Doolittle was on the way but he surprised them as he had done at Cleveland. He posed briefly for photographers while the plane was being gassed and, with several hours

Doolittle poses next to the Laird "Super Solution" which he borrowed to enter the cross-country race between Burbank, California and Cleveland, Ohio.
DOOLITTLE COLLECTION, AIR FORCE ACADEMY

of daylight left, he was back in the air and headed back to Cleveland. Later that evening, he and Jimmy Haizlip, a fellow Shell racing pilot, flew to St. Louis in the company Vega to attend a congratulatory party. September 4, 1931 had been a great day for Shell Oil Co., Jimmy Doolittle and aviation.

Jimmy was not through and wanted to race the Laird in the Thompson Trophy Race around the pylons to top off his accomplishments. He completed the qualifying course, along with seven other entries. Doolittle held up well during the race but during one lap, the engine began to lose power and smoke trailed from the Laird. With his engine overheating, Doolittle dropped out. The race was won by Lowell Bayles in a Gee Bee Z, designed by the Granville brothers.

To keep the company name and aviation before the public, Jimmy was authorized to make a series of record-setting flights between North American cities. He immediately established point-to-point speed records between St. Louis and other cities. He re-enacted the first airmail flight out of St. Louis, carrying a pouch of 5,000 letters and cut the old time in half to dramatize how much flying speeds had increased since earlier days when the government flew the mail.

The Bendix Trophy was awarded annually by the Bendix Aviation Corporation for the fastest speed in a coast-to-coast race beginning in 1931. Doolittle was the first recipient. The Bendix company held over 5,000 patents for automotive products at the time.
NATIONAL AIR & SPACE MUSEUM

A happy Jimmy Doolittle smiles for photographers after winning the 1931 Bendix Trophy Race from Los Angeles to Cleveland in the Laird Super Solution. He continued the flight to Newark, New Jersey to establish a new transcontinental speed record. He received a total of $10,000 for both feats. DOOLITTLE COLLECTION

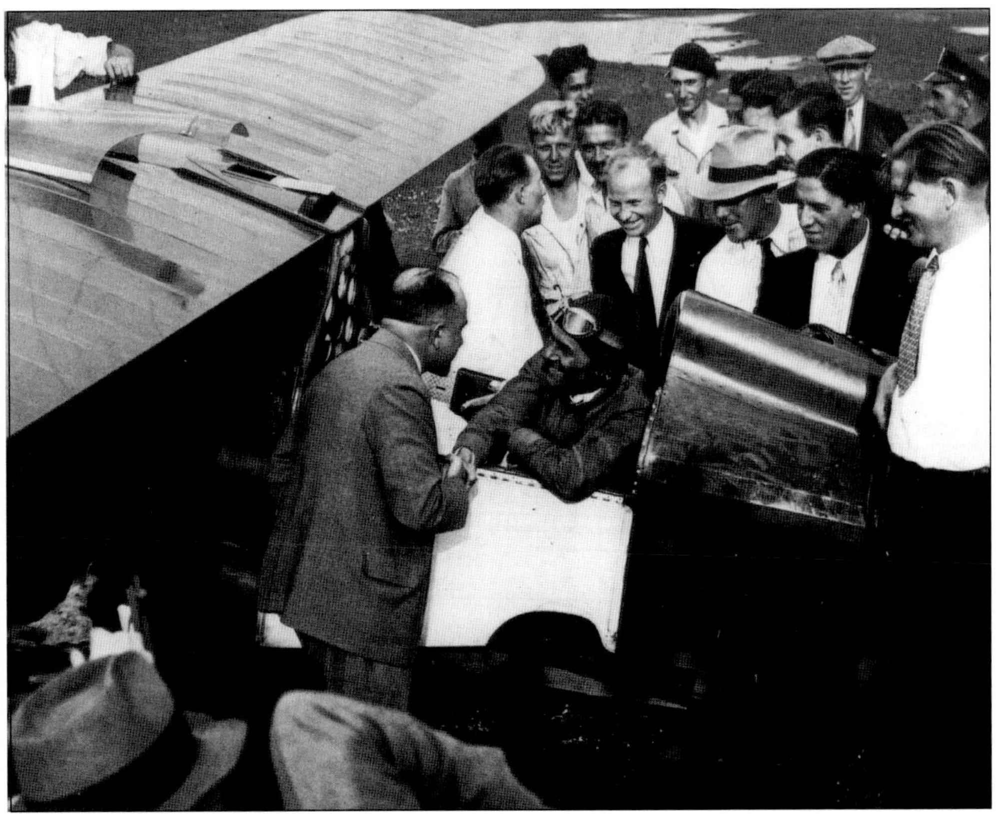

A tired Doolittle shakes hands with welcoming spectators at Newark after a coast-to-coast flying time of 11 hours, 11 minutes. He returned to Cleveland the same day and then proceeded to St. Louis to attend a celebration. DOOLITTLE COLLECTION

In mid-October, he few to Ottawa, Canada in the *Super Solution* and announced that he was going to fly to Mexico City by way of Washington, D.C. because no speed records had been set between the three national capitals. He took off from Ottawa, landed at Washington's airport, gassed up and flew to Birmingham, Alabama. After a seven-minute stop, he flew to Corpus Christi, Texas for a 16-minute gas stop and landed at the Mexican capital city 11 hours, 45 minutes flying time after leaving Ottawa.

After a week of warm Mexican receptions, Doolittle told his hosts he was going to set some more point-to-point records and did. He flew from Mexico City to St. Louis via Brownsville, Texas and Shreveport, Louisiana and touched down 6 hours, 35 minutes after leaving the 7,500-foot capital of Mexico.

The newspapers followed Doolittle's every move now. He decided to make a new type of flight to show that flying was becoming an increasingly safe and comfortable way to travel. He flew the Vega with Joe and two friends from St. Louis to Jacksonville, Florida for breakfast, had lunch in Havana, Cuba, and flew back to Miami for dinner. The flight made news, not because of the speed between each stop but because he deliberately made it look casual.

To capture more press attention, Shell publicists came up with a unique way to commemorate the 175th anniversary of the nation's postal service. The company purchased a Lockkeed Orion 9C Special and named it *Shellightning.* Could he fly it with two passengers and carry mail over all the routes covered by George Washington in his lifetime and do it in a single day? Doolittle looked over the route and thought it was possible. He would cover 14 states from Maine to North Carolina and west to Ohio. Commemorative mail would be dropped along the 2,600-mile route. Miss Anne Madison Washington, a descendant of the first president, would go along; Alphius F. Maple, an official of the Aeronautical Chamber of Commerce, would board at Newark, then all three would go to Boston for the official start.

Doolittle and Miss Washington departed Washington, D. C. on the morning of July 24, 1932, picked up Maples and flew to Boston. At 4:35 a.m. next day, with 30 bags of mail aboard, they flew to Kittery, Maine, the first mail drop-off point. It had no airport so a mailbag was thrown out the door. Doolittle swung south and repeated the mailbag drops at Portsmouth, New Hampshire; Providence, Rhode Island; New Haven, Connecticut; and Morristown, New Jersey. He landed at Washington, D.C. for gas. Fifteen minutes later, the Orion headed for Mount Vernon, Fredericksburg, Wakefield and Yorktown, Virginia, all towns with special meaning in Washington's life. The next mail was dropped at Sunbury, North Carolina. Turning north again, Doolittle flew over Christiansburg and Winchester, Virginia, then northwest to Fort Necessity and Pittsburgh, Pennsylvania where another gas stop was made.

Leaving Pittsburgh, the *Shellightning* flew to Point Pleasant and Pomeroy, Ohio, the point farthest west that Washington had ever traveled. Heading northeast now, Doolittle flew to Fort Le Boeuf, near Waterford, Pennsylvania, then to Rome, New York for a dusk mail drop. From there, it was on to Crown Point, Ticonderoga, Albany, and a final mail drop at West Point, home of the U. S. Military Academy. At 10:15 p.m., the tired trio stepped out of the plane at Newark. The flight had covered 2,610 miles in an elapsed time of 15 hours, 40 minutes from the time they dropped the bags at Kittery, the exact time Doolittle had figured it would take when he announced the itinerary and timing to the press.

Shell had prepared many post cards and letters with special cachets which were addressed to politicians and customers on a mailing list and mailed at the various drop points. Those that survive are very valuable today.

While the flight may have seemed like a publicity stunt, it proved a point for aviation. It was possible for a pilot to navigate to a number of towns, drop mail at any one of them, and do it on a reliable schedule. And it could be done with passengers on board.

Chapter 6

The End of the Racing Days

Just as the month of May means auto races in Indianapolis, September in the 1930s meant the National Air Races in Cleveland. In the months before the 1932 events, Doolittle's flying exploits had focused public attention on the races and pilots from many countries wanted to compete for the fame and fortune that came from winning the various events.

That summer, Jimmy announced his intention to enter the race for the Bendix Trophy again and hoped to lower the record he had set the year before. The *Super Solution* was rebuilt with some modifications and a larger engine. Most notable of the changes was the installation of retractable wheels which would fold up into the belly of the racer. He thought these changes would give him a top speed of 50 or 60 more miles per hour.

But fate intervened. On August 23, 1932, while flying it for the first time at Wichita, Kansas, he found that he could not crank the gear down. He wrote a note and dropped it to the ground crew: SOMETHING WRONG LANDING GEAR. I CAN GET THREE AND ONE-HALF TURNS BOTH WAYS. IF YOU HAVE ANY SUGGESTIONS, WRITE THEM ON SIDE OF PLANE AND COME UP OTHERWISE WILL USE UP GAS AND BELLY IN.

The ground crew hurriedly discussed what could be wrong and wrote on the side of a plane: ZOOM RIGHT, ZOOM LEFT, POWER DIVE. A pilot flew alongside and Doolittle waved. He tried all kinds of maneuvers to shake the gear loose but it wouldn't budge. When the gas was nearly gone, he made a wheels up landing on the belly

An unhappy Doolittle poses for photographers after reluctantly crash-landing the Laird *Super Solution* at the Wichita Municipal Airport when the landing gear failed to extend. He had hoped to fly it in the 1932 Thompson Trophy Race. The Granville brothers offered him their Gee Bee R-1 for the race. DOOLITTLE COLLECTION rather than abandon it and let it crash. It would take a long time to repair the damage; the *Super Solution* would not compete in any races that year.

It looked as though Doolittle's name wouldn't be among those competing for the Bendix trophy but offers to lend him a plane poured in from owners and manufacturers. One of the calls came from Zantford D. Granville, oldest of five Granville brothers, who offered him their Gee Bee R-1 racing plane, one of a line of hand-built racers. It was somewhat similar to the Model Z Super Sportster, flown by Lowell Bayles who had won the 1931 Goodyear and Thompson trophies. Jimmy flew to Springfield, Massachusetts to see about it.

As he walked around the Gee Bee, Jimmy wondered how such an airplane could fly. It looked like a barrel with its powerful Pratt&Whitney engine and short, stubby wings that seemed to be attached as an afterthought. There wasn't much of a vertical fin and there was just barely enough space in the cockpit for a small boy, and it was located just in front of the vertical stabilizer. Visibility for safe taxiing would be difficult.

As an aeronautical engineer, there was no doubt in Doolittle's mind that this plane would be fast but very unstable. The fuel tanks would not permit long flights so it wouldn't be the right plane for the Bendix cross-country race. He immediately decided he would enter the race for the Thompson Trophy instead. This race was around pylons spaced equally around a 100-mile triangular course.

"I flew the Gee Bee from Springfield to Cleveland," Doolittle told the author. "It was the touchiest plane I had ever flown and I didn't trust this little monster. It was fast but it was like balancing a pencil or an ice cream cone on the tip of your finger. You couldn't let your hand off the stick for a moment. I took it up to 5,000 feet and it's a good thing I did. It did two snap rolls before I could get it under control. If I hadn't had some altitude, I would have been dead. There was

The Gee Bee R-1 taxis in to the parking ramp for the Cleveland Air Races in 1932. Doolittle won the Clifford W. Henderson Trophy for the fastest qualifying time and also won the Thompson Trophy. He received $4,500 for winning the latter. AUTHOR'S COLLECTION

LAND PLANE RECORD IS SET BY DOOLITTLE

Flying Major Averages 296.287 Miles an Hour at Cleveland and Touches 309.04.

WILSON HURT IN COLLISION

Mrs. Haizlip Surpasses Women's Speed Mark—Husband Wins Free-for-All.

By LAUREN D. LYMAN.
Special to THE NEW YORK TIMES.

MUNICIPAL AIRPORT, CLEVELAND, Sept. 3.—Major James H. Doolittle established a world's land plane speed record here at noon today. Flying the Wasp-powered Gee-Bee racer from which he has obtained such tremendous speeds in the last three days at the National Air Races, he averaged 296.287 miles an hour. He made one course at 309.04 miles an hour. His achievement hoisted the world's speed record by about eighteen miles an hour.

no doubt I would have to fly this thing every second it was in the air."

Jimmy made some qualifying runs and hoped to set an official speed record but no barograph had been installed to ensure that a pilot did not exceed 1,300 feet altitude. He tried again and set an official record of 296.287 mph to win a prize of $1,575 for being the fastest qualifier.

When the race was about to begin, Doolittle found himself competing against the fastest fliers of that era. These included Colonel Roscoe Turner, James Wedell, Jimmy Haizlip, William Ong, Lee Gehlbach and others. Doolittle was the second off the ground in the timed departure sequence and quickly passed the first man off. Although every other pilot tried to catch up, it was Doolitle's race from then on. His speed was 252.686 mph and he pocketed $4,500 as the winner.

When the races were over, Doolittle returned the Gee Bee to Springfield. "I landed it, taxied up to the line and gratefully got out of it," he recalled. "That plane was the most dangerous airplane I ever flew." When asked why he would fly it if he knew it was so dangerous, he always replied, "Because it was the fastest plane in the world at the time."

Flying the Gee Bee in the 1932 race had a profound effect on Doolittle. Afterward, he learned that newspaper photographers had crowded around Joe and his sons waiting to take pictures of the expressions on their faces if he crashed. He felt that aviation had reached a state of maturity that it was time to examine the role of the air races in the furtherance of aviation. They had served a useful purpose by arousing public interest in aviation and many advances had been made in aircraft design and construction. But the price in planes and pilots had been high. Doolittle thought the time had come for aviation to serve world commerce rather than continue to be considered mostly a sport. "I have yet to hear of the first case of anyone engaged in this line of work dying of old age," he told a reporter.

A few weeks after the races, Jimmy made an official announcement that he was through with air racing. "We've learned a lot about engines and airplanes through racing," he said. "But it has come at great cost in lives and equipment. I think the time has come to give attention to safety and reliability. Commercial and military aviation must be developed so that we become strong commercially and have the best aerial fighting force in the world."

Many people did not believe Doolittle would retire from racing, but he never raced again. Instead, he devoted his time to testing and selling Shell aviation products. In the early thirties, most large aircraft engines used 91-octane gasoline. Although larger, more powerful engines could be designed, their increased compression required a higher octane rating for smoother burning and less detonation. Jimmy began a program of persuasion with the Shell chemists for the development of 100-octane gasoline. His argument was based on his knowledge that larger planes were being developed by the Army Air Corps at Wright Field, Ohio and engines of greater horsepower would be needed.

Shell officials had to be convinced that there would be a market if they developed 100-octane aviation fuel. It was the beginning of the Great Depression and funds were not readily available for new projects. Doolittle's argument was "No one else is doing anything about that demand when it comes. But it will come and we'll be ahead of the game."

Speaking as Dr. Doolittle, the scientist, instead of Jimmy Doolittle, daredevil racing pilot, enabled him to convince the officials at Shell and petroleum engineers began to design expensive new facilities. It wasn't an easy "sell" but a million dollar plant was built to produce 100 octane fuel at Wood River, Illinois which some Shell officials called "Doolittle's million dollar blunder." But, as Doolittle predicted, the larger, more powerful engines were soon built and the company was able to meet the burgeoning demand. It was one of Doolittle's major contributions to aviation.

As the country sank deeper into the economic recession, American industry looked abroad for business. The Curtiss-Wright Co. asked Shell to lend Doolittle to them for a round-the-world tour to demonstrate the Curtiss Hawk fighter plane. Shell agreed and in early 1933, Jimmy and Joe Doolittle began a five-month trip by ship that took them to the Philippines, Dutch East Indies, China, Japan, India and Europe. At each stop, Jimmy visited commercial and military facilities and put on his usual aerobatic show that left the spectators aghast. His fame had preceded him and people flocked to the airports to see him perform. Just as before during his two previous trips to South America, he was the best salesman for aviation products that Shell and Curtiss-Wright ever sent abroad.

Doolittle made a trip to China in 1933 for Shell and Curtiss-Wright. Shown at Peking are (left to right) Gen. Linson E. Dzau, Chinese military headquarters; Joe Doolittle; Mrs. Jack H. Jouett, wife of the former commander of the Chinese aviation school at Hangchow; Mark E. Moody, film producer; and Doolittle. DOOLITTLE COLLECTION, AIR FORCE ACADEMY

While the Doolittles had a delightful time personally, Jimmy obtained an unusual amount of information about aviation progress in the countries they visited. He was disturbed by some of what he saw. Countries that most Americans thought were backward were building air forces with substantial numbers of planes and pilots. Some were far ahead of America in research and development of new aircraft. Much emphasis was being placed on developing commercial airlines which would be of great benefit if a country's leaders decided to switch to military operations.

When Jimmy returned to the States, he decided to speak out about what he had seen and heard. Congress, by virtue of the Kelly Act of 1925, had taken the United States government out of the business of flying the mail and turned it over to business enterprises which marked the real beginning of scheduled commercial airlines in this country. Only mail was transported at first under government contract and pilots considered passengers a nuisance. However, as planes became more reliable, passengers were carried in ever-larger numbers. The government issued the mail contracts to those with the strongest financial backing. There were allegations of scandal which caused President Roosevelt to cancel all airmail contracts. The Army Air Corps, although not equipped and trained to fly scheduled runs in all kinds of weather, was ordered to carry the mail. In the ensuing weeks, there were a number of crashes, although only four fatalities occurred on actual airmail flights and these were primarily the result of the weather during one of the worst winters on record.

The public uproar that resulted caused the president to authorize new government contracts and the Air Corps resumed its Depression status with obsolete planes and inadequate funds for training pilots and crews. A Congressional investigation of the Air Corps was ordered and Doolittle was asked to serve on a committee to investigate all phases of the Air Corps and its military operations. There were 25 days of testimony by 105 witnesses, including generals, admirals, airline pilots, and specialists in engines, instruments, blind flying and meteorology. The gist of the plea of the 536 Air Corps officers who filed letters was in support of a separate air arm that would not be dominated by the ground-oriented generals and battleship-biased admirals.

The committee concluded its report by condemning the Air Corps officers who sought a separate budget, a separate promotion list, and freedom from the bias of the General Staff who accused them of disturbing "harmonious development and improvement." The committee noted that certain zealots had cultivated a fear that American aviation was inferior to that of the rest of the world and that this fear was unfounded.

The final report was concurred in by all the committee members except one. The lone dissenter, who asked for permission to file a minority statement, was Jimmy Doolittle. It said:

"I believe in aviation — both civil and military. I believe that the future security of our Nation is dependent upon an adequate air force. This is true at the present time and will become increasingly important as the science of aviation advances and the airplane lends itself more and more to the art of warfare. I am convinced that the required air force can be more rapidly organized, equipped and trained if it is completely separated from the Army and developed as an entirely separate arm. If complete separation is not the desire of the committee, I recommend an air force as a part of the Army but with a separate budget, a separate promotion list and removed from the control of the General Staff. These are my sincere convictions."

Disgusted by the board's narrow-minded conclusions, Doolittle replied to a reporter's question by saying, "The country will someday pay for the stupidities of these who were in the majority on this commission. They know as much about the future of aviation as they do about the sign writing of the Aztecs."

Doolittle continued to speak his mind in public in the years following. He warned that the Army Air Corps was extremely "weak in modern military aircraft and trained military pilots."

He stunned air racing enthusiasts in one speech by declaring that "air racing as a spectacle has outlived its usefulness." What was needed, in his opinion, was a new kind of racing—against the clock and in passenger/cargo planes. This kind of flying would enhance public confidence and prove that people and goods could go faster and safer from point-to-point.

To prove his point, Doolittle planned a race against time from Burbank to New York in an eight-passenger, single-engine Consolidated Vultee that he borrowed from American Airlines. He wanted to beat the coast-to-coast record set by Captain Eddie Rickenbacker of 12 hours, 3 minutes, 50 seconds on November 8, 1934 in a Douglas DC-1.

Jimmy invited his wife Joe and Robert Adamson, an official at Shell Oil Co., to go along as passengers. To take advantage of the high-altitude winds, he planned to fly at 15,000 feet which required oxygen for himself and passengers. He obtained a weather forecast and was advised that the best coast-to-coast weather with clear skies and tailwinds would be found on January 14, 1935. Trusting this prediction, Doolittle took off at dusk and flew all night without any navigational aids and mostly on instruments because the forecast was completely erroneous. Dead tired when daylight came next morning, he broke out of the clouds and could see the ground. He immediately recognized Richmond, Virginia and realized he was about 250 miles south of New York. He turned north, pushed the throttle forward and set the Vultee down at New York's Floyd Bennett Field after 11 hours, 59 minutes. It was only seconds short of an official speed record because of the requirement that a pilot had to beat a previous record by at least five minutes.

Doolittle was not pleased with himself and told the press that if he hadn't gotten off course, he could have been in New York an hour and a half sooner. However, he had achieved another aviation "first." It was the first time anyone had flown coast-to-coast non-stop in a transport plane with passengers in less than 12 hours.

Jimmy, Joe and a publicist flew a single-engine transport across the continent to set a record for passenger planes in 1935. Doolittle was first to fly coast-to-coast in less than half a day. DOOLITTLE COLLECTION, AIR FORCE ACADEMY

DOOLITTLE SPANS U. S. IN 12 HOURS

Breaks Old Record by Five Minutes in Hop From Coast With Passengers.

FLIES BLIND, BATTLES ICE

Wife With Him on Trip Made at Altitude of 16,000 Feet to Escape Clouds.

Flying blind and battling the flier's most dreaded hazard, ice, across the whole span of the continent, Major James H. Doolittle, breaker of many aviation records, set a new transcontinental mark for transport planes yesterday.

He set down the wheels of the American Airlines' Vultee eight-passenger plane at Floyd Bennett Field 11 hours 59 minutes out of Burbank, Calif. This broke by nearly five minutes the time of the Eastern Air Lines' Douglas, commanded by Captain E. V. Rickenbacker on its flight from Los Angeles to Newark last month. The record for racing planes is 10 hours 2 minutes, held by Colonel Roscoe Turner.

The pioneer of blind flying in this country had to put all his knowledge to the test to win safely through with his two passengers, Mrs. Doolittle and Robert Adamson of the California staff of the Shell Petroleum Products Corporation, for which Major Doolittle is aviation manager. It was, he admitted, the hardest flight of his experience, at least with the responsibility of passengers.

Clouds Miscalculated.

Studies of the weather map had promised good weather across the country before the take-off at 8:27 P. M. on Monday night. The skies were expected to be clear and the winds generally favorable above a local area of clouds. But the height of the clouds had been miscalculated and the low temperature caused the perilous ice formation that quickly coats the leading edge of a plane's wing, deforms it and adds hundreds of pounds to its load.

Lifting the craft laden with 600 gallons of gas from the Burbank field and driving swiftly upward, Major Doolittle found that the clouds extended thousands of feet higher than had been expected. Around 15,000 feet altitude ice started to form.

Swerving the plane to break up the ice formations, Doolittle drove it doggedly higher until, at 16,000 feet, it was nearly at its ceiling under full load. And there he had to hold it for most of the journey.

Times Wide World Photo.

AFTER BREAKING TRANSCONTINENTAL RECORD.

Major and Mrs. James Doolittle as they were welcomed yesterday by Mayor Ellenstein at the Newark Airport, where they flew from Floyd Bennett Field, after setting a new mark of 11 hours and 59 minutes for the trip from Burbank, Calif., to New York.

The Doolittles made many flights together for Shell Oil Co. to convince the public that flying was safe. Jimmy smiles from the cockpit of an American Airlines single-engine Vultee transport while "Joe" tries to maintain her balance on a ladder. DOOLITTLE COLLECTION, AIR FORCE ACADEMY

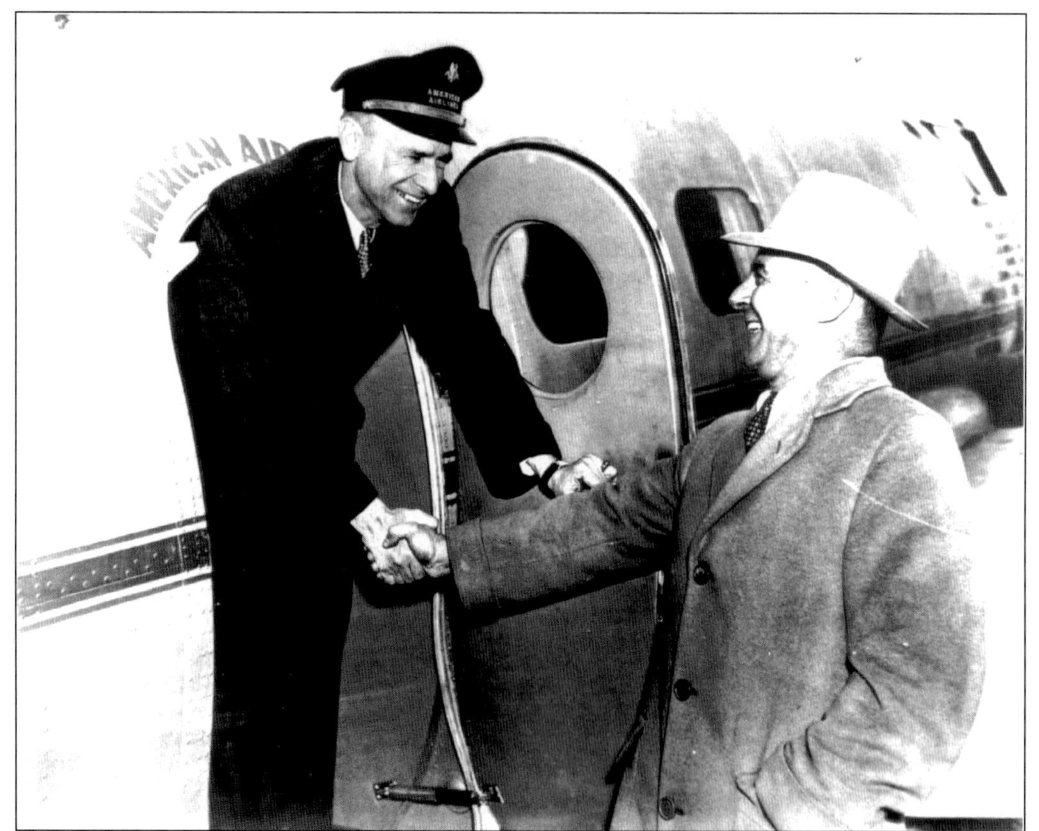

Jimmy congratulates Leland S. Andrews at Washington, D.C. An American Airlines pilot and his brother-in-law, Andrews had just set a new coast-to-coast speed record for transport planes in February 1935. DOOLITTLE COLLECTION, AIR FORCE ACADEMY

Honolulu Star-Bulletin 1st EXTRA

WAR!

SAN FRANCISCO, Dec. 7.—President Roosevelt announced this morning that Japanese planes had attacked Manila and Pearl Harbor.

OAHU BOMBED BY JAPANESE PLANES

Chapter 7

Back on Active Duty

The years after the 1935 coast-to-coast flight were busy ones for Doolittle. He gave many talks on aviation subjects and military preparedness and flew all over the country to visit aircraft manufacturers, aeronautical scientists and military personnel. He remained active in the Air Corps Reserve and served his annual two-week active duty tours as a major. His status as a respected scientist kept him abreast of the latest developments in industry and he received many awards during the period 1935-1940. He was named president of the Institute of Aeronautical Sciences in 1940, an honor reserved for those who have made genuine contributions to aviation progress.

There were disturbing activities taking place in Europe during this time. Adolf Hitler had taken over the government and a bloody civil war had taken place in Spain.

Jimmy went to Europe in 1937 on behalf of Shell and visited Ernst Udet, a famous World War I German ace. He spoke excellent English, loved to recite poetry, was a talented caricaturist, loved music and was a well-known crack shot with a pistol. The two had become friends at the 1931 and 1933 Cleveland Air Races where Udet put on daring aerobatic shows in a German-made Flamingo. Their friendship had enabled Doolittle to visit German aviation facilities and see that they were building hundreds of trainers, fighters and bombers, and had created the Luftwaffe, all in obvious repudiation of the treaties that had placed limitations on German armaments after World War I.

He rushed home and made many visits to spur American civilian and military officials into action to produce better planes and equipment. He continued to push for industry-wide development of 100 octane aviation fuel to meet the threat of war that he saw coming in Europe. But Americans were not thinking about a future war. They were still coping with the Depression and government funds were being devoted to carrying out the many "pump-priming" projects of the New Deal.

Jimmy returned to Germany in the spring of 1939. He found his old friend Udet was no longer the happy-go-lucky individual he knew before. He seemed embarrassed to have Doolittle around and didn't show him as much of the German aviation industry as before. However, Doolittle could see that military airplanes that were on the drawing board two years before were now on the flying line and hundreds of pilots had been trained.

Ernst Udet, German ace credited with 62 victories in World War I, performed daring aerobatics during the early Cleveland Air Races. He and Doolittle became friends and Doolittle visited him in Germany in 1937 and 1939. Udet, an outspoken critic of Hitler and Goering, died under mysterious circumstances during World War Two. DOOLITTLE COLLECTION

Ernst Udet drew this caricature for Doolittle in 1931.

By this time, Hitler had annexed Austria and taken over Czechoslovakia. The streets were filled with youths in uniforms who were fired up by Hitler's war preachings and anti-Jewish slogans. There was absolutely no doubt in Doolittle's mind that all of Europe would soon be ablaze in a new conflict that could easily turn into another world war because of the alignment of Germany, Italy and Japan.

Jimmy flew to London where he reported what he saw to the military air attache in the American embassy. It was quickly apparent that he did not share his concern and suggested that if Doolittle was so fired up about his observations to go back home and send a report to Washington. Furious at being so rebuffed, he returned to Washington and briefed his old friend and one-time commander at the War Department, Major General Henry H. "Hap" Arnold, then Chief of the Air Corps. Arnold listened attentively as Doolittle gave him information that substantiated what Lindbergh had told him on four visits he had also made to Germany. The difference in their views was that Lindbergh advocated isolation from being involved in European affairs. Doolittle was convinced that war was coming and the United States would be involved albeit reluctantly. He was so convinced by what he saw that he told Arnold he was willing to give up his job at Shell and serve full time or part time, in uniform or out, in any way he could be useful. Arnold was pleased but said he could not call anyone to active duty above the rank of captain until the beginning of the next fiscal year, July 1, 1940.

War did come to Europe on September 1, 1939 as 1,400 Luftwaffe planes bombed a stunned Poland. On September 3, Great Britain and France declared war on Germany. A week later, President Roosevelt declared a state of national emergency and decreed that the United States would become "the arsenal of democracy." France surrendered to the Nazis on June 22, 1940.

Doolittle was given an indefinite leave of absence from Shell and ordered to active duty as a major on July 1, 1940. His army pay was one-third of his salary at Shell. He was assigned to the Allison Engine Co. at Indianapolis, Indiana as assistant district supervisor of the Central Air Corps Procurement District. He asked for a P-40 fighter plane to be designated exclusively for him to make frequent visits between the manufacturers in his district, Wright Field in Dayton, Ohio and Washington. This was granted, along with a letter from Hap Arnold that gave him exclusive authority to obtain instrument clearances at his discretion in pursuit type aircraft. "This authority is granted in recognition of your exceptional qualifications," the letter said, "and to enable the Air Corps to obtain valuable information on the behavior and flying characteristics of modern pursuit-type airplanes under instrument conditions."

The Allison company had production difficulties with its engines that Doolittle found could be summarized with one word: dirt. He criticized the attitude of foremen and supervisors and made some individuals very unhappy but corrections were made. He admitted in his memoirs that, in the interest of national defense, someone had to be the "bad guy" and he was it.

In 1940, Doolittle volunteered to return to active duty as a major and was assigned to Detroit to assist in getting the automotive industry converted to wartime production. He is shown here with Edsel Ford (left) and Henry Ford. DOOLITTLE COLLECTION, AIR FORCE ACADEMY

Doolittle asked Arnold to send him to England in September 1941 to see how the British were coping under wartime conditions. He visited aircraft and engine manufacturers and flew several of the American aircraft they were getting from the United States, as well as the British bombers and fighters. There were a number of problems, the most serious of which was the absence of spare parts for the planes and accessories. The Royal Air Force and Navy wrote off 30 percent of their aircraft every six months, most due to crashes, not combat. Repairs were made to a dangerous extreme and pilots were flying aircraft badly in need of maintenance to a critical extent. Doolittle reported what he saw when he returned home and recommended changes that should be made in America's aviation industry and the Lend-Lease program.

There were problems in the U.S. automobile industry in converting to mass production of aircraft so Doolittle moved to Detroit. By the time of the Pearl Harbor attack on December 7, 1941, the industry had agreed on its terminal production of automobiles for the duration of the war that had been suddenly thrust upon the nation. Doolittle's wise counsel had helped to make the conversion to war production as smooth as possible.

The day before Christmas 1941, Arnold transferred Doolittle to Washington to serve on his staff as a "trouble-shooter." The role appealed to Doolittle because it meant he would not have to "fly a desk." He had missed one war and he didn't want to miss this one.

One of the first tasks Doolittle was given was to solve "the B-26 problem." The Martin B-26 Marauder was killing pilots because it never gave them a chance to make mistakes. Arnold wanted Doolittle's opinion if it should be continued in production or not. Doolittle gave one a thorough flight test and liked it. He felt that there wasn't anything about it that good piloting skill couldn't overcome. Pilots had to have more thorough instruction on flying the fastest medium bomber of that period. He recommended that it be built and it was.

Hap Arnold confirmed in his memoirs that he had sent Doolittle to a B-26 unit where there was concern about flying the airplane because of the number of accidents. He showed the pilots that flying the B-26 was no different from flying any other aircraft. "Before he left an outfit," Arnold said, "he had the boys flying the B-26 on one engine, making landings, and taking off with one engine, just as easily as they had formerly done with two."

When this task was completed, Arnold called Doolittle in and asked him, "Jim, what airplane do we have that will get off in less than 500 feet with a two thousand pound bomb load and fly 2,000 miles?"

The question had its origin from President Roosevelt who had asked his top generals and admirals to find some way as soon as possible to retaliate against the Japanese for the Pearl Harbor attack. An idea that might work came from Captain Francis S. Low, a submariner on the staff of Admiral Ernest J. King, Chief of Naval Operations. In early January, 1942, he had observed some Air Corps aircraft making simulated bombing passes at a Navy practice field near Norfolk, Va. where the deck of a carrier was marked off. He asked if it might be possible for Army bombers to take off from the deck of an aircraft carrier. Admiral King, also not a pilot, passed the question to his air officer, Capt. Donald B. Duncan who made some preliminary calculations and thought the B-25 might do it. King passed the suggestion to General Arnold who called for Doolittle.

Doolittle pondered Arnold's question and said he would come back with an answer. He narrowed the possibilities to the B-18, B-23 and B-25 if they could be modified to carry extra fuel. The next day, Doolittle said the answer was the B-23 or B-25.

"One thing I forgot to tell you," Arnold said, "The plane must take off from a narrow area not over 75 feet wide."

"Then the B-25 is the answer," Doolittle said. "The B-23's wing span would make it a close call. Now can you tell me why you asked the question?"

Arnold quickly passed on what Admiral King had told him. Essentially, the idea was a simple one in concept: The navy would load a few of the army's medium bombers on a carrier and take them within striking distance of Japan. The army pilots would take off, bomb military targets in the Japanese homeland, and fly to safety in China. Doolittle had unknowingly decided which bomber would be used. He agreed with Duncan's calculations but only if the carrier could make a minimum speed of 20 knots, which Duncan assured him it could.

Doolittle developed an immediate enthusiasm for the idea. "I need someone to take this project over, get the planes modified and train the crews," Arnold said.

"And I know where you can get that someone," Doolittle replied.

"O.K., Jim. It's your baby. You'll have first priority on anything you need to get the job done. Get in touch with me directly if anybody gets in your way." Doolittle immediately plunged into organizing what was destined to become one of the classic air operations of World War II.

Captain Duncan began planning for the Navy's part of the mission and proceeded to Hawaii. The *USS Hornet,* the Navy's newest aircraft carrier, was going through shakedown exercises off the Virginia coast. It would proceed through the Panama Canal and load the B-25s at Alameda, California on April 1. A 16-ship task force would be assembled, with eight ships departing from Alameda and the rest from Pearl Harbor, Hawaii and meet in the mid-Pacific. Complete secrecy was to be maintained or the Japanese would be lying in wait with their numerically superior forces.

One of the first activities was to assure that B-25s could indeed take off from a moving carrier. Two B-25s with a pilot and co-pilot for each plane were loaded on the *Hornet* and taken to sea off Norfolk. Both planes made it off easily.

While Duncan was preparing the Navy's plans, Doolittle had drawings made up for additional gas tanks in the B-25s and arrangements for them to be installed at Minneapolis, Minnesota. Special incendiary cluster bombs were manufactured at the Edgewater Arsenal in Maryland. Target folders were prepared in Washington and a decision was made to choose the pilots and planes from the three squadrons of the 17th Bomb Group and its associated reconnaissance squadron then being moved from Pendleton, Oregon to Columbia, South Carolina for sub patrol duty.

Word that volunteers were wanted for a special top secret mission was passed to the group and squadron commanders as they reported to

The *USS Hornet* (CV-8) in 1941. Only months after carrying the raiders to their launch point, the 20,000-ton carrier was sunk at the Battle of Santa Cruz. U.S. NAVY PHOTO

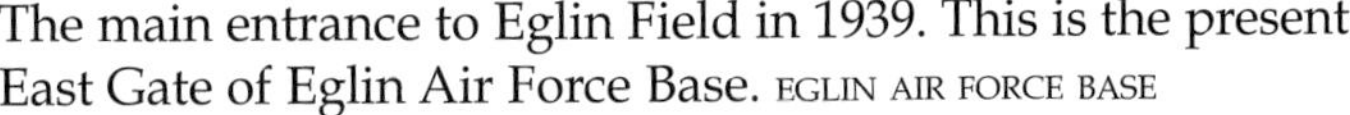

The main entrance to Eglin Field in 1939. This is the present East Gate of Eglin Air Force Base. EGLIN AIR FORCE BASE

their new station. Almost every officer and enlisted man volunteered so the squadron commanders had to decide who would go. Men and planes were flown to Eglin Field, Florida between February 27 and March 3, 1942. Meanwhile, Lt. Henry L. Miller, a flying instructor from Pensacola Naval Air Station, was assigned to teach the army pilots how to make short field takeoffs, a procedure that army pilots did not practice in their training in those days. Miller, who had never flown a B-25, was not told why he was doing this, although he suspected that it was for carrier takeoffs but did not realize that it was for the mission being planned.

There were armament problems that needed solving when the planes arrived at Eglin. Capt. C. Ross Greening solved several of them. He had two broomsticks painted black and placed them in the tail cones of all B-25s to appear as machine guns for any opposing fighter planes approaching from the rear. He also designed a simple "Mark Twain" bomb sight to replace the top secret Norden bombsight. It cost only 20 cents each to make them in the Eglin metal shops and worked far better at low altitudes than the expensive Norden. Each B-25 had one .50 caliber machine gun operated in the rear compartment by a power turret but most engineer/gunners had no experience with it and had to practice as much as time allowed. Bomb racks for the new incendiary bombs would not release properly and had to be reworked.

While the crews were wrestling with their problems, Doolittle continued to fly back and forth to Washington. When he met resistance from some quarter to get something done, he called Hap Arnold and the path was suddenly cleared. Arnold never questioned why or demanded an explanation. It was this authority that enabled Doolittle to get ready for departure from Eglin on time.

There was one question in Doolittle's mind that needed solving. He hadn't been told that he could lead the mission and pleaded for Arnold's permission. Arnold was reluctant but finally said that it was all right with him if it was all right with his chief of staff, Brig. Gen. Millard F. Harmon. Doolittle rushed to Harmon's office who said that if it was all right with Hap, it was certainly all right with him. That's all Doolittle needed to hear. As he rushed out of Harmon's office, he heard Harmon say, plaintively, "But Hap, I told him he could go." Doolittle hurriedly returned to Eglin.

During the third week of March 1942, a simple message was relayed from Hawaii to Washington: TELL JIMMY TO GET ON HIS HORSE. It was the signal for Doolittle and his men to proceed to the air depot at Sacramento, California.

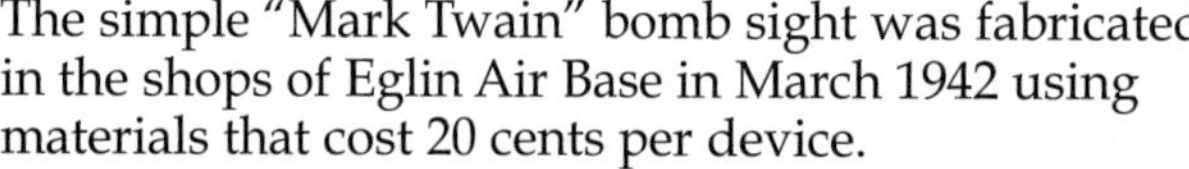

The simple "Mark Twain" bomb sight was fabricated in the shops of Eglin Air Base in March 1942 using materials that cost 20 cents per device.

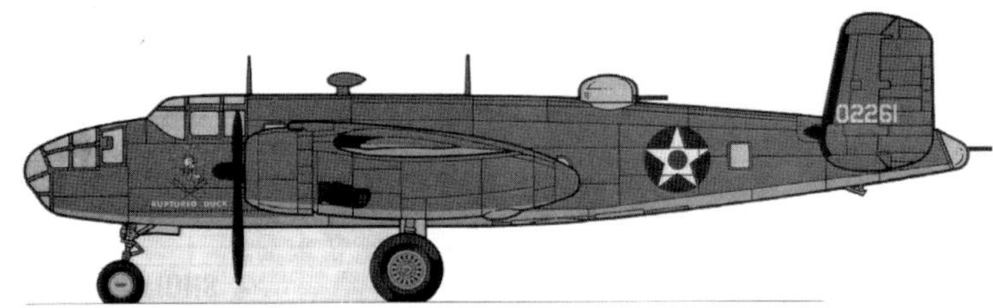

Chapter 8

The Raid on Japan

Twenty-two B-25s departed Eglin Field and proceeded individually to McClelland Field at Sacramento where they received maintenance check-ups and were then given quick test hops. They were flown to Alameda Naval Air Station on April 1, 1942 and towed to the side of the *Hornet* where 16 of them were hoisted aboard. The other B-25s were parked to be retrieved later by other Air Corps crews. The crews and maintenance personnel of all the B-25s filed aboard the carrier and were assigned to quarters. Doolittle had ordered that everyone must board the ship to have replacements for anyone who might drop out and also prevent information from being leaked out from anyone left behind.

On the morning of April 2, the *Hornet* and seven other ships sailed under the Golden Gate Bridge and headed west. When the force was out of sight of land, Capt. Marc A. Mitscher announced over the ship's intercom: "This force is bound for Tokyo!"

Doolittle called his men together and gave them all the essential details of their mission: the targets to be hit, escape and evasion information, and the expected defenses around the five target cities: Tokyo, Yokohama, Nagoya, Osaka, and Kobe. After dropping their bombs, they were all to head south, then west across the China Sea to fields in China where they would refuel and proceed to Chungking. Radio beacons would guide them to these fields. The danger was that Japanese forces had begun occupying China since 1937 and had steadily pushed their lines inland over the years of warfare. There was the possibility that the fields would soon be under enemy control.

For the next two weeks, the Army crews worked on their planes, reviewed their target folders and listened to first aid and sanitation lec-

Crew No. 1 for the raid on Japan consisted of (l to r) Lt. Henry A. Potter, navigator; Doolittle; Sgt. Fred A. Braemer, bombardier; Lt. Richard E. Cole, co-pilot; and Sgt. Paul J. Leonard, engineer/gunner. U.S. AIR FORCE PHOTO

Air crews gather around Lt. Col. James Doolittle and Capt. Marc A. Mitscher who are about to attach Japanese medals to a 500-pound bomb. U.S. NAVY PHOTO

This well-publicized photograph shows Doolittle wiring a Japanese medal to the fin of a 500-pound bomb on the deck of the *Hornet* before take-off for Tokyo. U.S. AIR FORCE PHOTO

tures by Dr. (Lt.) Thomas R. White, a physician who had volunteered to go on the mission as a gunner. Another eight-ship task force led by Admiral William F. "Bull" Halsey on the *Enterprise* joined the *Hornet*'s force at the 180th meridian. On April 10, Japanese intelligence officers intercepted "conversations" between the two task forces and calculated that they were heading for Japan and would be about 650 miles from Japan on April 14. However, they thought that the carriers would have to come within two hundred or three hundred miles of the Japanese coast before they could launch their scout and fighter planes. They had no idea there were medium bombers on the deck of one of the carriers.

On April 15, the carriers and cruisers were refueled and the oilers and destroyers withdrew. The closer the force got to the takeoff day, scheduled for April 19, the more the tension could be felt aboard the ship, especially as the weather deteriorated. Then it was realized the force would arrive at the takeoff point about 450 miles from the coast a day early. Doolittle was to take off at dusk, bomb his targets with incendiaries to light up the area for succeeding planes. But the plan was immediately changed early on the morning of the 18th when a scout plane from the *Enterprise* spotted an enemy surface ship only 40 miles away from the task force which was now 650 miles from Japan. Halsey immediately ordered a cruiser to sink the vessel and sent a message by light blinker: LAUNCH PLANES X TO COL DOOLITTLE AND GALLANT COMMAND GOOD LUCK AND GOD BLESS YOU

Mitscher then gave the order: "Army pilots, man your planes!" Doolittle grabbed his B-4 bag and sprinted to his plane as others followed. The carrier's deck was awash as the carrier's deck rolled and dipped in the wind. Doolittle started his engines and moved to the starting position. As the launching officer signaled, Doolittle revved up both engines to full throttle and released the brakes when the officer's flag went down. He was airborne within a few yards with plenty of deck to spare. It was 8:20 a.m.

At right, a Japanese surface vessel that was spotted by a scout plane. This sighting forced the Doolittle crews to take off early and farther from Japan than had been planned.

Capt. Marc A. Mitscher, skipper of the *USS Hornet*, watches Doolittle take off before reaching the end of the deck on his way to bomb Tokyo. All 15 planes followed successfully but a sailor was injured when he fell into a spinning propeller of the last plane. Three Doolittle Raiders died the day of the raid and eight were captured by the Japanese in China. U.S. NAVY PHOTOS

The 15 other planes followed one by one for the next hour. One pilot had difficulty when he inadvertently placed his flaps in the UP position but managed to maintain his airspeed and gradually climbed out safely. As the last airplane was starting its engines, a sailor slipped on the wet deck into the spinning propeller and had to have his arm amputated.

Halsey's task force immediately turned back toward Hawaii. Soon after, three patrol planes ditched, two men were lost; three more planes were damaged in landing accidents.

Doolittle's planes continued westward to their respective targets individually. Only two or three saw any other B-25s. The weather improved as Doolittle arrived over Tokyo around noontime just as an air raid drill was being concluded. There were fighter planes in the air but none attacked his B-25. Several of the planes that were following dodged ships and an enemy patrol plane en route but were apparently unnoticed.

Doolittle and 14 following planes dropped their bombs and headed southward to avoid flying over land until they reached the southernmost Japanese islands before turning west towards China. One plane, however, apparently had exceptional fuel consumption and the pilot decided to head for Russia after dropping his bombs, rather than risk a ditching. He landed on a field near Vladivostok where he and his crew were forbidden to gas up and proceed to China. The plane was confiscated and the five men were interned for nearly 14 months.

The 15 planes heading toward China ran into headwinds and it seemed certain they would all run out of fuel and have to ditch in the sea, despite their best efforts at reducing fuel usage. Slowly, as the hours dragged on, the headwind turned into a slight tailwind and all were able to make the mainland. However, the weather turned sour and darkness obscured the landscape. Four pilots decided to ditch their planes in the water or land on or near the beach, while others climbed through the weather and continued over the mountains until their fuel ran out. These crews bailed out into the rain and darkness.

Of those who elected to crash-land their planes, four members of one crew were severely injured; on another, two men drowned while swimming to shore. One man on a third plane died attempting to bail out. Eight crew members of two other planes were captured by the Japanese.

Thirteen of the crews that had made it to the Chinese mainland evaded the Japanese and made their way to Chungking. There, Doolittle kept score on his men as they made their way to safety. When he learned that two crews had been captured, he promptly offered ransom to have them released if held by guerrillas and tried to persuade the Chinese general in the area to send troops to their rescue. There was neither enough money nor enough troops to get them back. The Japanese had eight captives and intended to wreak their vengeance on them for what their propagandists immediately branded as an "inhuman, insatiable, indiscriminate bombing attack on Japanese hospitals, schools, and homes." Three of these men were executed by a firing squad in October 1942; one died of malnutrition the following year. The remaining four survived forty months of torture, starvation and solitary confinement and were liberated by American troops in August 1945. (Their complete story can be found in *Four Came Home* published by Pictorial Histories Publishing Co.)

Doolittle was heartbroken when he learned of the deaths and captures. He had lost all of his planes, including the one that had landed in Russia. He fully expected to be court-martialed for failing to carry out the second half of his mission: deliver the planes to American units then being formed in China. He was genuinely surprised in Chungking when "Hap" Arnold wired congratulations on his promotion from lieutenant colonel to brigadier general, skipping the rank of colonel.

The effect on Allied morale was exactly what was needed at this most dismal time in American history. The news spread around the world that not only had Tokyo been bombed successfully by American planes but that the raid had been led by Jimmy Doolittle. When headlines proclaimed TOKYO BOMBED, it was the best news for depressed Americans that could be imagined. Not only had the Japanese capital been bombed, but it had been a surprise attack carried out exactly as the enemy had done at Pearl Harbor—from aircraft carriers and without loss to the naval units that made the raid possible.

While news of the daring retaliatory attack spread around the globe, Doolittle was ordered

Doolittle sits dejected beside the wreckage of his B-25 on a Chinese hillside after he and his crew bailed out. He believed the mission was a failure because 15 of the crews had to bail out or crash-land and the 16th plane and crew were interned in Russia. U.S. AIR FORCE PHOTO

Wreckage of Doolittle's plane which crashed north of Chuchow. Chinese soldiers are examining the wreckage. U.S. AIR FORCE MUSEUM COLLECTION

Doolittle and his crew with Chinese officials. From left, S/Sgt. F.A. Braemer; S/Sgt. Paul Leonard; General Ho, director of the Branch Government of Western Chekiang Province; Lt. Dick Cole; Doolittle; Henry H. Shen, bank manager; Lt. Hank Potter, and Chao Foo Ki, secretary of the Western Chekiang Province Branch Government. U.S. AIR FORCE PHOTO

Madame Chiang Kai-Shek, wife of China's World War II leader, reads the citation for the medals she had just presented to Doolittle and Maj. John A. Hilger. Doolittle had just been promoted to brigadier general, skipping the rank of colonel. U.S. AIR FORCE PHOTO

MORNING EDITION

Japan Times & Advertiser

Incorporating
The JAPAN CHRONICLE and The JAPAN MAIL

(THE 17th YEAR of SHOWA) TOKYO, SUNDAY, APRIL 19, 1942

9 ENEMY RAIDERS DOWNED

Japanese Annihilate Remnants in Cebu; Passi Is Captured

Ensign of Imperial Navy Flies Over Iloilo, Panay Isle

U.S. LOSSES HUGE

NEW STATE POLICY OUTLINED BY PIBUL

Responsibility of Maintaining Independence Rests on People, Says Premier

AUTARCHY EMPHASIZED

Imperial Family Absolutely Safe In First Air Raid Over Capital

DOG-FIGHTS STAGED IN AIR OVER CAPITAL

Army Machines Intercept and Shoot Down Invading Enemy Planes

BARRAGE BALLOONS UP

Damage By Incendiary Bombs Small; Planes Repulsed

WARNINGS SOUNDED

"Enemy planes, coming from several directions, attacked the Keihin district at about 12:30 p.m. today. The invaders, counter-attacked by our air and ground defense forces, are in gradual retreat. The enemy planes so far ascertained to have been shot down number nine. The damage suffered by us seems to be slight. The Imperial Family is in absolute security."

Foreign News Spotlight

Exclusive Flashes

Copy of Tokyo newspaper published in English the day after the Tokyo Raid. It contained various propaganda stories such as nine enemy (U.S.) planes being shot down, dogfights over Tokyo, and anti-British feeling increasing in the U.S.

The day after the raid, the Tokyo English-language newspaper, *Japan Times and Advertiser*, contained propaganda about the raid. Of course, no planes were lost over Japan. U.S. AIR FORCE MUSEUM COLLECTION

"All the News That's Fit to Print."

The New York Times.

LATE CITY EDITION

Section 1

VOL. XCI—No. 30,766. NEW YORK, SUNDAY, APRIL 19, 1942.

KOBE AND NAGOYA BOMBED, JAPANESE SAY; FIRE DAMAGE LAID TO 60 'AMERICAN' PLANES; U. S. PLANES RAID RANGOON, CHINESE RETIRE

M'NUTT MADE HEAD OF A NEW BOARD TO RULE MANPOWER

Sweeping Order Gives Him the Power to Issue Directives to Many Federal Agencies

EVEN DRAFT IS INVOLVED

Nelson Will Be On the New Commission—Hillman Named Special Aide to President

By FRANK L. KLUCKHOHN

City's Ocean Front Ordered Darkened

FIRE BLAZES AGAIN IN NORMANDIE HOLD

Caused by an Acetylene Torch, Smoky Blaze Is Put Under Control in 3½ Hours

FOE IS HIT IN BURMA

Japanese Fail to Halt Demolition of Oil Wells in Yenangyaung Area

FLANKED CHINESE RETREAT

British Will Not Leave Field to Allies, but Are Anxious to Real Tired Troops

By DAVID ANDERSON

PLACES JAPAN SAYS WERE BOMBED AND POSSIBLE AVENUES OF APPROACH

SOVIET UNION

MANCHUKUO

KOREA

HONSHU

PACIFIC OCEAN

HAWAIIAN ISLANDS

PHILIPPINES

BORNEO

TOKYO ADDS DETAIL

Insists Raids on 4 Cities Hit No War Targets in Two-Hour Assault

BASE IS STILL A MYSTERY

But Japanese Suspect Carrier, Expect New Blows—Indicate Damage to Transport Lines

U.S.-MEXICAN BOARD FIXES OIL AWARDS

$23,995,991 Sum Indicates We Agreed Subsoil Rights Did Not Belong to Companies

R. A. F. Hammers Hamburg; 7 of Augsburg Raiders Lost

By CRAIG THOMPSON

LAVAL FILLS SLATE; TAKES FOUR POSTS

Becomes Chief of Government Under Authority of Petain, Who Broadcasts Today

By LANSING WARREN

OIL THEFTS LINKED

Section 4

REVIEW OF THE WEEK

EDITORIAL CORRESPONDENCE

WEEK-END CABLES

The New York Times.

EDITORIALS

LETTERS TO THE EDITOR

SPECIAL ARTICLES

Section 4

SUNDAY, APRIL 19, 1942.

THE NEWS OF THE WEEK IN REVIEW

Bombs on Japan

U. S. Strikes Back

UNITED STATES BOMBERS TAKE THE WAR TO THE JAPANESE

Alert in Tokyo

Across Mountain Trails

Leahy Called Home

Laval in Vichy

A Move by Hitler

Tired Wehrmacht?

Columbus Evening Dispatch

OHIO'S GREATEST HOME DAILY

Associated Press News, Wide World Features, Wirephotos
International News Service

VOL. 71, NO. 292. *** Telephone—MAin 1234 COLUMBUS, OHIO, SATURDAY, APRIL 18, 1942 16 PAGES PRICE 3 CENTS

U.S. WARPLANES RAIN BOMBS ON LEADING CITIES OF JAP EMPIRE

YANK BOMBING PLANES CARRY WAR TO ENEMY

(By The Associated Press)

AMERICAN bombers lashed at the Axis on far-flung battlefronts today, and military observers estimated that the Allies were throwing nearly 3000 first line warplanes against the enemy every 24 hours.

Informed sources declared the vast new aerial offensive was beginning to wrest the initiative in sector after sector on all war fronts.

With American assembly lines rolling off an endless stream of fighters and bombers, these were today's proofs of their punching power:

1. Planes identified as American bombed Tokyo and other Japanese cities for the first time in history.
2. U. S. army bombers operating from bases in India pounded Japanese-occupied Rangoon, Burma, a key springboard for enemy naval operations in the Bay of Bengal and for the land drive in Burma.
3. American-built Boston (Douglas) planes joined in the RAF's non-stop offensive against the German-occupied French "invasion coast."
4. Allied warplanes, presumably including United States aircraft, again blasted Japanese-held Koepang, in Dutch Timor, where the Japanese have been massing for attacks on Australia.

"America is becoming a deciding factor in the war," a London military expert said, pointing to the widespread raids.

"For the first time, she is actually placing an effective number of planes in distant fighting lines, which means that the battle of production and transportation is being won.

"From now on, it's going to be planes, planes and more planes in India, Egypt, Britain, Australia, China and every other battlefront until the initiative everywhere is ours.

"Japan threw her maximum strength in the initial attacks. Her air position cannot improve. Germany and Italy have shown a steady decline in their air strength since last year."

Tokyo, Yokohama, Kobe And Nagoya Hit in Big Three-Hour Offensive

(By the Associated Press)

TOKYO, (From Japanese Broadcasts), APRIL 18.—The Japanese command announced that hostile warplanes bombed Tokyo, Yokohama, Nagoya and Kobe today and caused air-raid alarms to run through three of the four main islands of Japan. Observers said the raiders over Tokyo bore the insignia of the United States air force.

(The Japanese embassy in Buenos Aires, Argentina, issued a communique saying flatly that the attacking planes were American.) The raids began at 12:30 p. m., Tokyo time, and the all clear was not sounded until three hours and 20 minutes later, the communique said.)

These were the first air raids in Japan's experience.

(Thus in one tremendous sweep, the attackers, in what appears to have been the most daring air assault in history, struck at the heart of the Japanese empire; at Tokyo, the capital, population 7,000,000, the world's third city; Nagoya, 1,400,000, center of the aircraft industry; Kobe, 1,200,000, chief port of the empire, shipping point for supplying the Japanese armed forces in the southwest Pacific; Yokohama, 950,000, the port for Tokyo.)

Raid alarms were in force for varying periods from the northern tip of Hokkaido to Shikoku in the south, including most of the main island, Honshu. (This embraces a sweep of more than 1000 miles.)

Imperial headquarters announced that raiders which "approached from several directions" came over the Tokyo - Yokohama area half an hour after noon and that two hours later two planes raided Nagoya and a

CHUNGKING, APRIL 18.—(AP).—It was learned on most reliable authority tonight that today's air raids on Japan were not based in China. This strengthened belief that an aircraft carrier was used.

single raider dropped incendiaries on Kobe. The latter is 376 miles west of Tokyo.

Official announcements said that "it is confirmed thus far that nine enemy planes were shot down" in the Tokyo-Yokohama area and that in all cases the damage was light.

(The claim of nine raiders destroyed suggests a raid by a total of many times that number.)

"Observers declared that without doubt the planes which bombed the Tokyo-Yokohama region were United States machines," said the Tokyo radio. "They said the American blue star ensign could be seen clearly from the ground."

Communiques of eastern defense headquarters, in Tokyo, and central defense headquarters, in Osaka, showed that the following regions were under raid alarms for varying periods during the afternoon:

All of Hokkaido, northernmost of the main islands; the Tohoku district, the eastern coast of Honshu above Tokyo; the Tokyo-Yokohama area; the Tokaido, the thickly settled belt along Honshu's southeastern coast between Tokyo and Osaka; the Kyoto-Kobe-Osaka triangle, industrial heart of the empire; the Chugoku district, around Okayama and extending almost to the western tip of Honshu; the island of Shikoku, south of Honshu.

Late in the afternoon it was announced that the western defense headquarters, which includes the fourth of the main

Continued on Page THREE, Column ONE

HUNDREDS OF BUILDINGS REPORTED WRECKED IN RAID ON JAPS

Tokyo was playing air raid when this picture was taken. Smoke from a practice incendiary fire rises from the plaza directly in front of Tokyo's main railway station. Japanese civilians have been trained by such demonstrations for several years in preparation for the real thing that happened Saturday. (AP). Wirephoto.

In another rehearsal for the air raid that finally came members of the women's fire-fighting brigade are pictured in an air-raid drill on the Ginza, Tokyo's Broadway. This drill took place before the war with the U. S.

(OTHER TOKYO PICTURES ON PAGE 2-3)

Japanese reports Saturday revealed that warplanes, identified as American, had raided (1) The Tokyo-Yokohama area and the cities (2) of Nagoya and Kobe. The Berlin radio reported a fire of unannounced origin destroyed more than 400 buildings and killed a number of persons in Oguni (3) The raid caused air raid warnings across 800 miles of the Japanese archipelago. (AP). Wirephoto.

United Nations On Offensive In Far Pacific

WASHINGTON, APRIL 18.—(AP).—Chairmen of the house military and naval committees maintained today that the bombing of Japanese cities, as described by Tokyo, meant the start of an offensive war by the United Nations in the Far Pacific.

"It is the beginning of a general offensive," asserted Representative May (D) of Kentucky, chairman of the military committee. "While it is hard for me to believe anything Japan says, this bears out my prediction of 10 days ago that Tokyo would be bombed shortly."

Representative Vinson (D) of Georgia, chairman of the naval committee, elated by the report of the aerial attacks, declared that "it appears to me that the Allied nations are beginning to take the offensive."

Although Tokyo said its observers were convinced the raiders were United States warplanes, the army and navy here said they had no confirmation of the reported foray.

Assuming Tokyo to be telling the truth, there are several explanations of the lack of confirmation. If the raiders operated from an aircraft carrier, there would be no reports from the United States forces until their radios could be operated without disclosing ocean positions the enemy would like to know. Thus, the raid of a United States task force on Wake and Marcus islands was not officially announced here for weeks afterwards.

$500,000 IN WAR BONDS IS DUE U. S. FLYERS IF TOKYO BOMBING IS CONFIRMED OFFICIALLY

CHICAGO, APRIL 18.—(INS).—Riches—$500,000 or more in war bonds — will be showered upon some American flyer, or group of flyers, if the government officially confirms that American planes have bombed Tokyo.

Ever since Japan's stab-in-the-back on Pearl Harbor, Dec. 7, American Legion posts, clubs and patriotic groups from coast-to-coast have been purchasing war savings bonds and setting them aside for the first American to drop a bomb on Tokyo.

Some of the awards were designated for the first bombing of the Japanese capital by any United Nations flyer. Conservative estimates put the total of the prizes at more than $500,000.

The Rev. Preston Bradley of Chicago is custodian of one $1000 bond purchased by John L. Keeshin, proprietor of a trucking firm, "for the first American flyer to bomb Tokyo—and may he get it soon."

"The bombing of Japanese cities will sacrifice lives, but it also will save millions of lives later in the war," the Rev. Mr. Bradey said. "Force is the only language the Japanese understand."

Authorities on army and navy law disagreed as to whether officers and men could accept the many prizes offered. Should it be interpreted that they cannot, most of them are expected to go to USO and army and navy relief organizations.

BUY WAR BONDS

TRANSFER OF $2,000,000 TO AID DEFENSE SOUGHT

Governor Would Make Poor Relief Surplus Available to Aid Local Defense Councils.

First steps to set up a state "defense relief fund" from which local defense councils will be allocated funds to carry on civilian defense work will be taken Monday when Governor Bricker will request authority from the Ohio control board to transfer a $2,000,000 surplus from the state poor relief fund to the new fund.

If approved, the money would be allocated to the various local defense councils on the basis of the tax duplicate of the municipality over which they have jurisdiction and would be used only to carry on civilian defense activities.

Franklin county would receive approximately $119,400 under the program.

Resolution asking the transfer of the surplus, consisting of $1,500,000 saved in 1941 and $500,000 which it is estimated will be saved this year, was passed at a meeting of the 16-member state defense council Saturday morning. Governor Bricker heads the Ohio council.

The governor said that such a transfer of funds had been declared legal by the attorney general office. Four of the five control board members must approve before the transfer can be made. Members of the board are the state finance director, the state auditor, the attorney general and the chairmen of the house and senate finance committees.

BUY WAR STAMPS

Light Frost Forecast For Columbus Tonight

With temperatures running about 10 degrees below normal Saturday morning, the forecast warned Columbus residents that cooler weather was in store for Saturday night, with light frost if the sky cleared. There was no frost Friday night, the weather bureau reported.

Friday's maximum temperature was followed by a low of 40 degrees at 6 a. m. Saturday. At noon the mercury stood at 45.

BUY WAR STAMPS

NOTED CONDUCTOR DIES

SAN FRANCISCO, APRIL 18.—(AP).—Alfred Hertz, 69, composer and symphony orchestra conductor, authority on Wagnerian interpretation, died today.

Fire Hits Store At Worthington

Blaze Is Witnessed by Hundreds of Spectators.

While hundreds of spectators watched, firemen from Columbus and Worthington brought under control a blaze in Kroger store in High street at Worthington early Saturday.

The fire started in an electric hot plate and firemen broke out the front showcase windows to fight the blaze. While the loss was not officially estimated, officials said the floor and a large meat case were badly damaged.

A ladder and pump company from Columbus went to the scene to aid the village department in fighting the fire.

BUY WAR STAMPS

NAVY MAY TAKE OVER OPERATION OF AIRPORT

Possibility that the navy will take over operation of Port Columbus, possibly by May 1, was seen Saturday following a conference Friday afternoon between city officials and a navy representative.

Although Mayor Green and Service Director Grover Clements would not comment on the meeting, discussions apparently centered on a lease agreement between the city and the navy which may be offered to council Monday night.

It also was reported that the city is prepared to offer the navy an alternate site for a base near the Greenlawn avenue bridge if the government decides not to take over the municipal airport.

It is doubtful, however, that the river itself would be of value for seaplane operations because of its winding nature and comparative shallow depths.

Two Courses Open

Should the navy decide to lease the municipal airport, two courses of action are open:

1. The field might be designated as a military airport in which case all commercial flying, both airlines and private, would be banned and the control tower would be manned by navy men.
2. The field might be designated a joint military-civilian airport in which case the control tower would remain under the jurisdiction of the civil aeronautics authority while the field itself would be under control of the navy.

At Louisville, where a similar arrangement exists, the CAA is in charge of the control tower

Continued on Page THREE, Column ONE

BUY WAR STAMPS

HIT-SKIP VICTIM

While crossing South High street near Frankfort street, early Saturday, Donald W. Long, age 23, of 103 West Sixth avenue, was struck by an auto and suffered ankle and chest injuries. He was taken to St. Francis hospital. Police said the driver of the car failed to stop after the accident.

Increase in Lend-Lease Aid to Russia Reported

WASHINGTON, APRIL 18.—(AP).—The White House today reported a sharp upsurge of lend-lease aid to Russia, saying that two and a half times as much was sent in March as was sent in February

Late War Bulletins

BERLIN, APRIL 18.—(By Official German Wireless)—(INS).—New air raid alarms sounded in various areas of Japan this afternoon, according to the German news agency DNB.

Tokyo had a new alarm at 3 p. m., while the sirens also were sounded in Kyoto, North Osaka and Okayama, 70 miles west of Kobe.

Alerts also were sounded in central Japan from coast to coast.

ROME (FROM ITALIAN BROADCASTS), APRIL 18.—(AP).—An Italian destroyer has sunk a submarine in the central Mediterranean, the Italian high command announced today.

* * * BUY WAR BONDS * * *

Cebu Falls to Jap Invaders; City Is Reported in Flames

WASHINGTON, APRIL 18. — (INS). — Lieut. Gen. Jonathan M. Wainright reported today that despite continuing fierce resistance by his outnumbered forces, the city of Cebu, second largest in the Philippines, has fallen to the enemy and is reported to be burning.

This was disclosed in a war department communique which also stated that the aerial bombardment and shelling of Corregidor is continuing, but that the defenders have blasted Jap-held roads and bridges on Bataan, disrupting enemy communications.

Fierce resistance also was reported on the important island of Panay, where the Japanese landed recently, apparently in an effort to "cash in" finally on the riches of the Philippines.

to Washington via India, North Africa and South America. He was instructed to avoid the press and was whisked to his Washington apartment and told to remain there out of sight until General Arnold called him. The call came on May 20.

"Jim," Arnold said, "Put on your cleanest uniform. I'm going to pick you up in about 20 minutes."

Doolittle dressed hurriedly and bounded out the door of the apartment house when the olive-drab army sedan drove up. He grinned at Arnold in the back seat, now wearing the three stars of a lieutenant general, and noticed there was another officer in the rear seat with him. It was General George C. Marshall, Army Chief of Staff.

Doolittle saluted and exchanged greetings with the unsmiling Marshall and got in the front seat. As they pulled away, he asked where they were going and Arnold told him they were going to the White House. "The President is going to give you the Medal of Honor," he said.

Doolittle twisted quickly in the seat with a surprised look on his face. "That's ridiculous, sir! I don't deserve the Big Medal."

Arnold was surprised at Doolittle's reaction and frowned. Marshall stared at Doolittle and said quietly, "I happen to believe you do." Nothing more was said.

Upon arrival at the president's outer office, Doolittle received his second surprise when a side door opened and in stepped his wife, Joe. Neither could believe their eyes. They had not seen each other since they bid goodbye in San Francisco six weeks before and Joe had no idea what Jimmy had been doing. She had received a call from Arnold asking her to fly from California to Washington on a top priority pass. She could not imagine why haste was so necessary. When she arrived at Washington National Airport, a driver and an officer met her with a limousine and rushed to the White House.

President Roosevelt greeted the four of them warmly, then said, "Jimmy I'm proud of you. All America is proud of you and as their president, it is my privilege to present you with the Medal of Honor."

Jimmy leaned forward as the president pinned the medal on his shirt. "Thank you, Mr. President," was all he could think of to say. Although he accepted the award graciously from his commander-in-chief, he did not think he deserved it. He always said he accepted it on behalf of all the men who shared the same risk he did. The citation accompanying the award summarized the reason he received it:

> For conspicuous leadership above and beyond the call of duty, involving personal valor and intrepidity at an extreme hazard to life. With the apparent certainty of being forced to land in enemy territory or to perish at sea, General Doolittle personally led a squadron of Army bombers, manned by volunteer crews, in a highly destructive raid on the Japanese mainland.

Lt. Gen. Henry H. "Hap" Arnold, chief of the Army Air Forces, jokes with Doolittle shortly after the Tokyo Raid in 1942. They had known each other since the early 1920s when Arnold was base commander at Rockwell Field, San Diego, California.
U.S. AIR FORCE PHOTO

President Roosevelt pins the Medal of Honor on Doolittle with Joe Doolittle, General Henry "Hap" Arnold (behind Roosevelt) and General George C. Marshall, Army Chief of Staff, looking on. U.S. AIR FORCE PHOTO

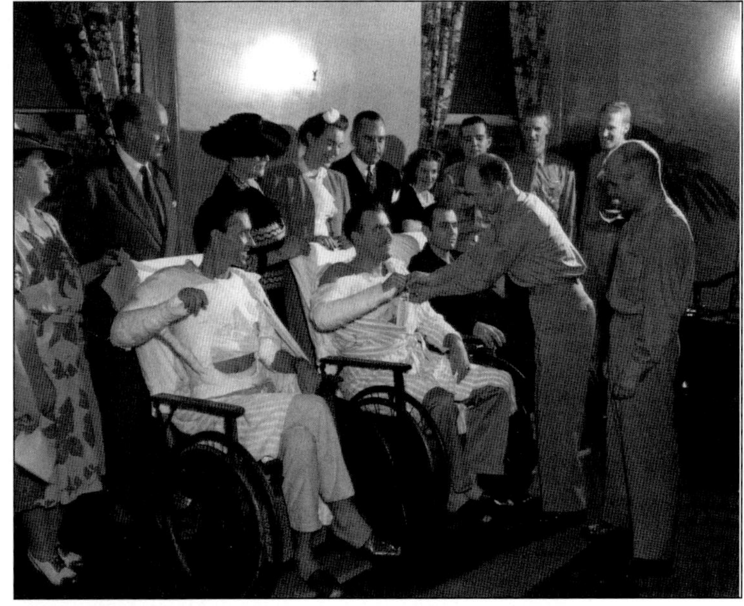

In the first such ceremony conducted at Walter Reed Hospital in Washington during the war, Maj. Gen. Millard F. Harmon, chief of staff of the Air Force, pins the Distinguished Flying Cross on 1st Lt. Harold F. Watson. To Harmon's left is 1st Lt. Charles L. McClure; to his right, 1st Lt. Ted W. Lawson. General Doolittle looks on. In the background are Secretary of the Treasury, Henry Morganthau (second from left) and parents and wives of the raiders. Two additional raiders, 2nd Lt. Howard A. Sessler (far right) and 1st Lt. James M. Parker, Jr. (second from right), were also present. U.S. AIR FORCE PHOTO

Scene at Bolling Field as 25 of Doolittle's Raiders were presented the Distinguished Flying Cross. Lt. Gen. Henry "Hap" Arnold is pictured pinning the coveted medals on the men. U.S. AIR FORCE PHOTO

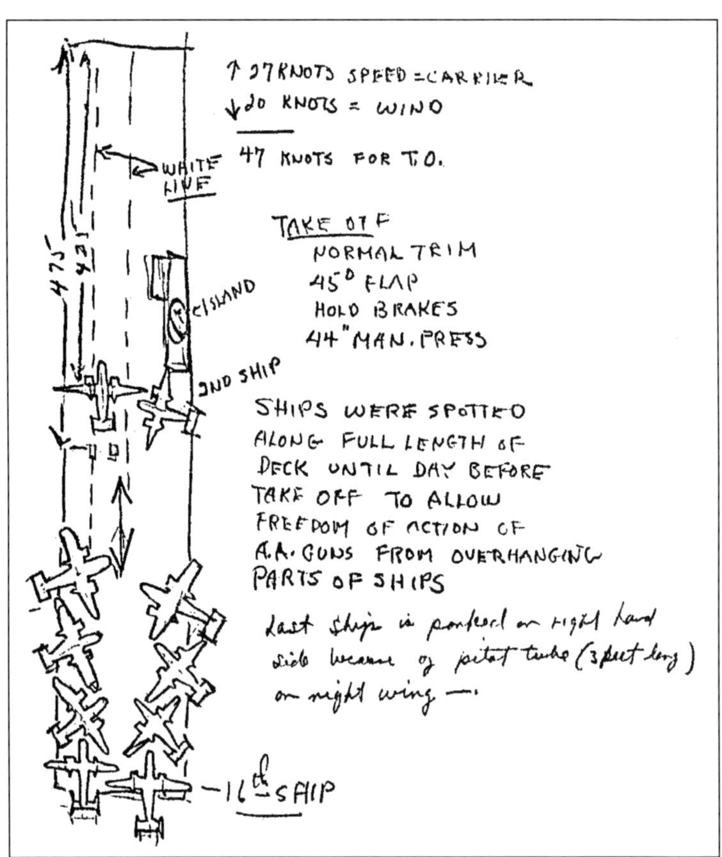

From the "Report on the Aerial Bombing of Japan" by Brig. Gen. James H. Doolittle, U.S. Army, June 5, 1942.

An informal reunion of Doolittle and some of his Tokyo Raid volunteers was held in a farmhouse in North Africa on April 18, 1943, the first anniversary of their mission. Not all of those pictured were on the raid; some were available on the carrier as spare crew members. Four Raiders later became prisoners of the Germans. U.S. AIR FORCE PHOTO

A promise Doolittle made on the carrier to give the Tokyo Raiders a party after the raid was finally fulfilled in Miami, Florida, in December 1945. Here at their second reunion in April 1947 are (l to r, front row) Carl Wildner, Robert Bourgeois, Joseph Manske, Doolittle, David Jones, Ted Lawson, Everett Holstrom. (Seated, rear row) Thomas Griffin, William Pound, George Barr, unidentified medical attendant for Barr, and Horace Crouch. U.S. AIR FORCE PHOTO

General Doolittle receives a plaque containing a fragment of the B-25 "Whirling Dervish." Alexander Burton, right, of North American Aircraft Co. made the presentation at the 1947 Miami Beach reunion. U.S. AIR FORCE PHOTO

The Doolittle Raiders met on April 18, 1947, at Miami Beach, five years after the historic raid. U.S. AIR FORCE PHOTO

Reunions of the Doolittle Raiders have been held each year since 1947 except 1952 and 1966 because of the Korean and Vietnam wars. Doolittle and his Raiders pose for their annual reunion photograph at St. Petersburg, Florida in 1982. U.S. AIR FORCE PHOTO

The Raiders gather at General Doolittle's interment at Arlington National Cemetery, October 1, 1993. PICTORIAL HISTORIES PUBLISHING COMPANY PHOTO

The silver goblets shown below were donated by the citizens of Tucson, Arizona as a tribute to Doolittle's Raiders. They are taken to the reunions each year and used to toast the crew members who are no longer living. The deceased are represented by the goblets that are turned down. The goblets are displayed at the Air Force Academy between annual reunions. AUTHOR'S COLLECTION

Chapter 9

On to North Africa

It was several years before historians could assess the full impact that the Doolittle raid had on the Japanese. Neither General Arnold who approved the mission nor Jimmy Doolittle who flew it, nor President Roosevelt, who presented him with the Medal of Honor, would have dared to predict that not only would the raid cause confusion and impede war production briefly and give Americans a tremendous morale boost but would also have a much greater effect on the future of the war. The Japanese war strategy in the Pacific was changed as a result of this single air action. It encouraged the Japanese to engage American air and naval forces at Midway two months later in which they suffered their first major defeat at the hands of the United States.

The Battle of Midway marked the turning point for Japanese strategy during World War II. The Doolittle Raid had encouraged the Japanese to over-commit themselves and underestimate the ability of American air and sea power to fight back. The extraordinary risk taken by Jimmy Doolittle and his 16 crews, plus the 10,000 men in the Navy task force of 16 ships was indeed justified.

When the news was released that Jimmy Doolittle had been awarded the Medal of Honor, he was hounded by newsmen for details. The President had told the press that the planes had departed from Shangri-La, the mythical country made famous by James Hilton in his novel *Lost Horizon* and many details were withheld for nearly a year. Eight men were in the hands of the enemy and no one knew what suffering they would have to endure if all the facts were made known.

To take advantage of the morale boost that Doolittle had given the nation, General Arnold encouraged him to visit defense factories around the country, make radio talks and give talks of encouragement. The theme was that America had struck back after the attack on Hawaii and more attacks were to come.

When the Tokyo Raid moved off the front pages, Arnold called Doolittle to his office one day in August 1942, to announce that he was recommending to Gen. Dwight D. Eisenhower, commander of American forces in England, that Doolittle be assigned to organize and command the Twelfth Air Force which was being activated at Bolling Field, Washington, D.C. An invasion was planned for North Africa and the Twelfth would carry the war to the Axis forces that were occupying the entire region.

Eisenhower balked at the nomination. He had never met Doolittle and knew about him only through newspaper stories of his air racing victories and dare-devil aerobatics. Doolittle had never commanded any unit larger than the 100 volunteers he had trained for the retaliatory attack on Japan. He had been out of the service for 10 years and Eisenhower thought anyone who had been away from the military that long would not be up to date on the administrative details and operational requirements of large combat units. Meanwhile, orders were issued transferring Doolittle to Eisenhower's headquarters in England.

The two men had a long conversation when Doolittle reported for duty. The meeting was cordial but did not go well. Afterward, Eisenhower sent messages to Arnold and Marshall that he did not want Doolittle and preferred men he had known before such as Generals Carl "Tooey" Spaatz, Ira Eaker, or Tony Frank, three bomber specialists who had served during World War I and had never left the service. Arnold and Marshall replied jointly that he could have anyone he wanted but they still recommended Doolittle. Eisenhower did not respond but reluctantly accepted him and adopted a wait-and-see attitude. Doolittle immediately went about the task of overseeing the movement of hundreds of men and planes to invade North Africa and begin operations against the Germans and Italians.

The invasion of North Africa began on November 7, 1942. Doolittle's forces established themselves along the northwest portion of Africa. Although the landing operations were successful, Doolittle almost didn't get there. Four days before the first Americans were to go ashore, he flew to Gibraltar as a passenger aboard a lightly armed B-17. The plane flew without an escort offshore parallel to the coast of France which was believed to be out of the range of enemy patrol planes.

The flight was uneventful until the B-17 was suddenly attacked by four Junker Ju-88s. The B-17 pilot immediately dropped to the wave tops. Bullets laced through the bomber's fuselage as the enemy planes took turns attacking. No vital parts were hit but the co-pilot was wounded. Doolittle, standing in the radio compartment during the attack, rushed forward and helped the navigator ease the co-pilot out of his seat. After helping to give him first aid, Doolittle slipped into the co-pilot's position. The young pilot, a lieutenant, asked Doolittle, now a two-star general, if he wanted to take the controls.

"It's your airplane, son," Doolittle said. "You're doing a good job."

The encounter did not last much longer. The German planes, probably low on gas, broke off the attack and the B-17 continued to Gibraltar. Doolittle was able to enter two hours of co-pilot combat time in his log book. It was his first brush with the enemy.

During the next three months, the Twelfth Air Force made history. Doolittle's task was to build an air force from scratch in the desert sands of Africa. Once ground troops were landed, there was no turning back. In the crowded weeks that followed, his bombers pounded German General Erwin Rommel's forces unmercifully and destroyed their lines of communication and supply. Doolitle, who believed in seeing every aspect of operations himself, was everywhere. He refused to have an aide assigned and when he flew a B-26 to visit his units, he had Sgt. Paul Leonard, his mechanic on the Tokyo Raid, along as a co-pilot.

In March 1943, the War Department announced that Doolittle had been awarded the Air Medal for bombing missions against the enemy. Once more, he became front page news. But war correspondents who tried to locate him found only that he was everywhere and nowhere. His executive officer would only say that his boss did not know what chairs were made for because he never sat down.

In the early months of the war in North Africa, the going was difficult. The Germans put up heavy flak over every target and many American bombers fell to their destruction. The toll of the fliers was heavy and those who survived began to dread the next mission. Morale sank to a dangerously low point.

Their leader was well aware of this as he talked with returning crews. When they spoke of how tough a mission was, Doolittle would nod, give a word of encouragement that the mission had done some good against the enemy, and move on. To the surprise of most, they found that Doolittle had flown on the very mission they had described. As crews went to their aircraft, it was his custom to displace a co-pilot on a plane scheduled to fly somewhere in a formation, sometimes at the "tail-end Charlie" position or elsewhere so he could observe their formation, their air discipline and the offensive tactics of enemy fighters.

Doolittle (third from left) flew 25 combat missions while commanding the Twelfth Air Force in North Africa. He often chose to fly with a crew just before departure to observe the air discipline of his own forces from different positions in a formation and the fighter tactics of the enemy. U.S. AIR FORCE PHOTO

The aircraft he flew in were hit by enemy flak and fighters several times but he wasn't wounded. When word got around that their leader was no desk-bound general, morale improved and so did the teamwork so necessary in air combat.

Doolittle made it a point to check out in every type of aircraft in his command. He used a British Spitfire and P-38 fighter planes for quick trips between bases but flew the twin-engine B-25s and B-26s, as well as four-engine B-17s from the pilot's seat on actual bombing missions. The young pilots quickly learned that "the Old Man" was no desk general.

During the middle of the North African campaign, Doolittle experienced what he described as "my greatest personal tragedy of the war." He had landed at a forward airdrome and left the airplane, a B-26, in the care of his faithful crew chief Sgt. Paul Leonard, who had been his engineer/gunner on the Tokyo Raid. While Doolittle was having a conference in the nearby town that night, German fighters strafed the field. Leonard manned the plane's machine gun turret and fired at the attackers as long as the batteries held out.

Doolittle found the plane next morning but Leonard was not in it. He had held out as long as he could and then leaped into a nearby bomb crater. A bomb had landed in the crater and the faithful engineer who had been with him in China was killed.

In the following weeks, as his bombers had their effect on the enemy supply lines, the German resistance began to crumble. Doolittle's crews stepped up attacks on the island of Sicily and on Italy itself. He flew on raids against military targets in Rome and added the second of the three Axis capitals to his list of enemy capital targets. He hoped that he could participate in missions against Berlin, Germany's capital city.

The tiny island of Pantelleria was the target of Operation Corkscrew which Doolittle wanted to be a significant mission: it would be the first attempt to conquer enemy territory with air power alone. Located between Africa and Sicily, it had to be captured before Sicily and Italy could be invaded. Only 42 square miles in area, it had only one harbor and no beaches on which barges could be landed easily. Photo planes had located over 100 gun emplacements in strategic positions. German heavy flak guns were in place all over the island and Doolittle ordered his fighters and bombers to attack the island with everything they had. Heavy bombers came at high altitudes and dropped their heavy bombs on large targets such as supply dumps. Medium bombers came in lower and aimed at the smaller targets. The fighters strafed anything that moved. On D-Day, leaflets were dropped offering the Italians a chance to surrender unconditionally but there was no response.

Ships loaded with troops left North Africa and Malta and prepared to go ashore on the night of June 10-11, 1943. British warships maneuvered into position and the first assault landing craft began the run to the coast. However, Doolittle's pilots reported that a white cross had been painted on the runway of the island's only airport. A large white flag flying from a hill overlooking the harbor was seen by the invasion force. The Italians had surrendered to Allied air power before a single American went ashore!

Not all of Doolittle's missions were so successful. He recalled one of them as "the most unsuccessful mission I ever participated in." It began with a report that the Italian battleship *Roma* and two large cruisers were located in the harbor at Spezia. It was important that they be prevented from leaving to go out and attack Allied naval units. Three B-17 groups of about 100 planes were assigned to the effort. One group was to attack the *Roma*, the other to go after the two cruisers. All planes carried 1,600-pound armor-piercing bombs and 2,000-pound demolition bombs. Doolittle tells what happened:

"I led the operation and the flight in and out was fairly uneventful. When we developed reconnaissance pictures after the mission, we found that one cruiser hadn't been hit at all and the other had only a forward gun turret knocked off by a 2,000-pound bomb. The *Roma* itself had an armor-piercing bomb go through the hull and come out the bottom without exploding.

"Although three groups had been put on the raid to be sure the job was done, we had accomplished virtually nothing. This was a disturbing revelation. What made it worse was that weeks later, after Italy had surrendered, the *Roma* left the harbor to be turned over to the British at Malta. Near southern Italy, a single German dive bomber dropped two radio-controlled bombs and sank it."

Despite this one failure, Doolittle had exhibited a personal brand of leadership and success by this time that did not go unnoticed in high places. He had shown that he could lead men and that he could get along with his ground and naval counterparts. His reward came in the form of a short note from General Eisenhower. It said:

Dear Jimmy:

When you joined me in London you had much of what it takes to exercise high command. I am not exaggerating in any sense when I tell you that in my opinion you have shown during the past year the greatest degree of improvement of any of the senior United States officers serving in my command. You have become a soldier in every sense of the word and you are, every day, rendering services of inestimable value to our country and to the United nations.

Sincerely,
Eisenhower

Doolittle, then a major general, receives his first Distinguished Service Medal from General Dwight D. Eisenhower in North Africa in 1943. U.S. AIR FORCE PHOTO

Jimmy was pleased, even more so when he received the Distinguished Service Medal from his commander in a private ceremony.

There was more in store for Doolittle. When the Tunisian campaign was over and the Italians had surrendered, more strategic missions were flown against the Germans. It was decided to divide the Twelfth Air Force into two air forces. The Twelfth would become a tactical air force and support the army advancing northward in Italy and during the planned landings in southern France. As of November 1, 1943, the Fifteenth Air Force would be the new strategic air force and concentrate on bombing industrial targets on the Italian mainland still under German control and in Austria and southern Germany that could not be

Lt. Gen. Mark Clark (left) and Maj. Gen. John K. "Joe" Cannon pose with Doolittle after the American invasion of Italy in 1943. U.S. AIR FORCE PHOTO

reached from England. Many of the aircraft and men to fill the billets designated for the new air force were transferred from the Eighth Air Force in England which did not please Gen. Ira C. Eaker, then its commander. Doolittle was designated commander of the Fifteenth and moved his headquarters to Bari, Italy where another surprise awaited him. He and Eaker were to change places. He was assigned as commander of the Eighth Air Force and Eaker was named commander of the Mediterranean Allied Air Forces with the 12th, 15th, British desert and Balkan air forces under him. Doolittle officially took over the Eighth on January 6, 1944 and was promoted to lieutenant general in March. He thus became the first Army reserve officer in history to attain three stars.

Doolittle decorates Brig. Gen. Hoyt S. Vandenberg informally in North Africa for his service as Twelfth Air Force chief of staff in 1943. Vandenberg became Chief of Staff of the U.S. Air Force in 1948. U.S. AIR FORCE PHOTO

Bob Hope shows "Joe" Doolittle photos he took while on tour in North Africa during World War II. DOOLITTLE COLLECTION, AIR FORCE ACADEMY

Chapter 10
The Mighty Eighth
and
Return to Civilian Life

The "Mighty Eighth" Air Force had reached a turning point in its history with Doolittle's assignment. General Eaker had built it from scratch since August 1942 with a few bombers but was never able to overwhelm the enemy's defensive forces. The Eighth was dedicated to daylight bombing of specific targets with precision while the British bombed large areas at night. Eaker had great losses because he had not been given the forces he needed in time. By the time Doolittle arrived, many more units had been sent and long range fighters were being introduced to accompany the bombers for protection to distant targets. The strategy of the bombing campaign was to prepare for the invasion of the continent in June 1944.

Doolittle did not change his methods of command when he arrived in England. He was always on the move visiting all of his units between war conferences with his boss, General Carl "Tooey" Spaatz, and intelligence briefings. He had acquired an aide but still didn't want one. Doolittle wanted to fly on missions with his men but was forbidden to fly over the continent while the enemy held it because he had been briefed and given access to Ultra, the code-breaking system that permitted the Allies to eaves-drop on top secret German messages. Anyone knowing about Ultra could not risk being captured. Besides Doolittle had been briefed on invasion plans. He was never to realize his desire to bomb the third Axis capital.

One story told about Doolittle during this period shows his aggressive style of leadership. He was visiting the office of Major General William E. Kepner, head of the 8th Fighter Command, and saw a sign on the wall:

> THE FIRST DUTY OF THE EIGHTH AIR FORCE FIGHTERS IS TO BRING THE BOMBERS BACK ALIVE.

Doolittle asked where that sign came from and Kepner replied that it was on the office wall when he got there. Doolittle told him to take it down and put up another one to read:

> THE FIRST DUTY OF THE EIGHTH AIR FORCE FIGHTERS IS TO DESTROY GERMAN FIGHTERS.

"You mean you're authorizing me to take the offensive?" he asked.

"I'm directing you to." Doolittle responded.

Kepner, a fighter pilot, was pleased. He had been asking permission to do that for months but had not been given permission to leave the bombers to pursue enemy fighters to their bases. From that time on, American fighter pilots took the offensive as they had not done before. While some fighters always covered the bombers, the bulk of the fighter force now went aggressively after the German interceptors in the air and on the ground.

As the fighters stepped up their attacks, the bombers shifted their targets to the German petroleum industry since fuel was a Luftwaffe prime necessity. The increased bombing tempo, as Allied units pushed across France after the invasion of June 6, 1944, played havoc with the enemy's efforts to move men and war materials to the front lines. By March 1945, it was obvious that the complete collapse of the German army was not far off.

Toward the end of the assault on Germany, bombing by the use of radar was being perfected. This permitted bombardiers to attack targets covered by clouds. However, it was not as accurate then as now and best results were always achieved when targets could be bombed visually.

On one important mission, a formation leader was ordered to proceed to an alternate target if he thought the primary target was covered by clouds as he approached it. But the primary target was more important of the two and the clouds did not seem to be breaking up. He was about to divert to the alternate target when he got a radio

U.S.

At left: This photo, taken after Doolittle's return from the Far East in 1945, features his famous grin. The six stripes on his left sleeve indicate that he spent three years overseas during World War II. In addition to the ribbon indicating that he had been awarded the Medal of Honor, others show the Distinguished Service Cross, Silver Star, Distinguished Flying Cross, Bronze Star, Air Medal and decorations from Belgium, China, Ecuador, France, Great Britain, and Poland. DOOLITTLE COLLECTION, UNIVERSITY OF TEXAS, DALLAS

Working out a simulated navigation problem while Doolittle and Brig. Gen. Edmund W. Hill watch is Lt. Lloyd Peterson, B-17 navigator. The photo was taken at a Combat Crew Center in England where newly arrived crew members studied the latest methods developed in actual combat. U.S. AIR FORCE PHOTO

Doolittle greets King George VI and Queen Elizabeth as the royal couple pays a visit to Eighth Air Force headquarters in 1944. U.S. AIR FORCE PHOTO

Princess Elizabeth, Great Britain's future queen, listens intently while Doolittle briefs her during a visit with her parents to an Eighth Air Force base in 1944. Doolittle was later awarded a decoration as Knight Commander, Order of the Bath, for his wartime service to England. U.S. AIR FORCE PHOTO

Many women "manned" the civil defense air warning centers during World War II. Mrs. Doolittle is shown how military and civilian aircraft are tracked as they pass over an area on the eastern seaboard. DOOLITTLE COLLECTION

Mrs. "Joe" Doolittle learns how to become a "Rosie, the Riverter" as hundreds of workers and guests look on during her tour of an aircraft plant during World War II. DOOLITTLE COLLECTION

Mrs. Doolittle smashes a bottle of champagne on the bow of a new ship at an unidentified Navy yard during World War II. She traveled widely to give talks to war industry employees, and wrote a syndicated column for wives of servicemen. U.S. NAVY PHOTO

"Joe" Doolittle hosts a CBS radio show during World War II. Her guest is Eleanor Roosevelt, wife of the President.
DOOLITTLE COLLECTION, AIR FORCE ACADEMY

"Joe" Doolittle, shown here wearing her husband's Command Pilot wings, built up a large corps of listeners during the 14 months she had a regular matinee radio show during World War II. Listeners were inspired by her sincere, concerned messages of hope and patriotism. One of her themes was that wives and sweethearts should not insist on knowing what their men were doing or where they were going because they had neither a need nor a right to know.
DOOLITTLE COLLECTION, AIR FORCE ACADEMY

During World War II, "Joe" Doolittle participated in many ceremonies to promote aviation. Here she places a flag decal on the nose of the *City of Washington*, a United Air Lines DC-3. DOOLITTLE COLLECTION

Jimmy, "Joe" and John Doolittle unite when Jimmy returns from the war in Europe after a three-year absence. John was a cadet at West Point and took pilot training there. He remained in the Air Force for a full career and retired as a colonel. DOOLITTLE COLLECTION, AIR FORCE ACADEMY

A former test pilot in the 1920s, Doolittle prepares for a test flight in a Lockheed P-38 Lightning in England that had been having carburetor trouble. One engine caught fire on takeoff but Doolittle landed safely. U.S. AIR FORCE PHOTO

King George VI, accompanied by Doolittle, reviews a military police force during a visit to an Eighth Air Force base "somewhere in England" during World War II. U.S. AIR FORCE PHOTO

Doolittle checked out in the B-29 Superfortress in preparation for the Eighth Air Force's anticipated participation in the bombing of Japan. However, the Eighth's bombers did not fly any combat missions against the Japanese. U.S. AIR FORCE PHOTO

Doolittle hosts King George VI, Queen Elizabeth and their eighteen-year-old daughter, Princess Elizabeth, at the christening of *Rose of York*, an Eighth Air Force B-17 Flying Fortress, after the 1944 D-Day landing. U.S. AIR FORCE PHOTO

Brig. Gen. Charles Y. Banfill (l), Director of Intelligence, and Maj. Gen. Orvil A. Anderson, Deputy Commander for Operations, confer with Doolittle on an upcoming Eighth Air Force mission to Germany. The background map shows a mission with primary and secondary targets indicated. U.S. AIR FORCE PHOTO

The crew of an Eighth Air Force B-17 brief their commanding general on the course they will fly on their upcoming bombing mission over Germany. Doolittle was forbidden to fly on combat missions over German-occupied territory after being briefed on Germany's secret war code. U.S. AIR FORCE PHOTO

Capt. James H. Doolittle, Jr. is decorated with the Distinguished Flying Cross by his father in 1944. The younger Doolittle had earned the award for service in the Pacific Theater before being assigned to duty in the Eighth Air Force. U.S. AIR FORCE PHOTO

Secretary of the Treasury Henry Morgenthau, Jr. during a wartime visit to North Africa looks on as Doolittle points to the cartoon on the nose of a B-17 Flying Fortress. U.S. AIR FORCE PHOTO

Gen. Carl A. "Tooey" Spaatz autographs a "short-snorter" bill for Doolittle at a dinner marking an 8th Air Force unit's 100th mission over Europe. Those who had flown across the ocean were entitled to "membership" in the mythical Short Snorter Club. U.S. AIR FORCE PHOTO

Lt. Gen. Carl "Tooey" Spaatz, Gen. George Patton, Doolittle, Maj. Gen. Hoyt S. Vandenberg and Brig. Gen. Otto P. Weyland line up for photographers at an advance headquarters "somewhere in Europe" during the final days before victory in Europe. U.S. AIR FORCE PHOTO

Gen. Dwight D. Eisenhower, supreme Allied commander, congratulates Doolittle after awarding him an Oak Leaf Cluster to the Distinguished Service Medal, January 25, 1945. Officer in the background is Maj. Gen. Frederick L. Anderson, member of Doolittle's staff, who also received the DSM. U.S. AIR FORCE PHOTO

Lt. Robert Lynch, operations officer, assigns a P-38 to his commaing general for a flight to visit one of the Eighth Air Force combat units in England. Doolittle flew every type of aircraft assigned to his squadrons. U.S. AIR FORCE PHOTO

Gen. Carl A. Spaatz (l), commander of U.S. Strategic Air Forces in Europe, and Doolittle listen as a bomber crew tell of their experiences on a mission just completed. Doolittle flew over the beachhead on D-Day in a P-38 and was first to brief General Eisenhower on what he saw. U.S. AIR FORCE PHOTO

Doolittle shares a joke with his superior officer, Gen. Carl A. Spaatz, somewhere in England in 1945. Both men had known each other since the early 1920s. U.S. AIR FORCE PHOTO

message that the primary target could be seen. He continued and found the clouds had parted and the bombs were dropped.

Colonel Budd J. Peaslee, one of Doolittle's bomber pilots, had proposed that a fighter with a wing man be sent ahead of the bombers and report the weather. Doolittle approved the idea and directed the organization of the 1st Scouting Force equipped with P-51s. Many bomber pilots also liked the idea and volunteered to switch to fighters. The concept paid off in fewer missions canceled, lower accident rates and lives saved.

Doolittle had another idea that was not so well-received. He suggested to General Arnold that the number of missions before a bomber crew member could go home be increased from 25 to 30. He also suggested that experienced crews should expect to be returned to combat after a period of rest in the States. His reason was that bomber crews reached a high rate of effectiveness at 25 missions and were replaced with inexperienced crews. It took a while to demonstrate but the survival rate improved in direct proportion to bombing accuracy as the Eighth continued its assault on Hitler's Third Reich.

The results of the attacks against the enemy by the Eighth Air Force have been examined closely by historians. In the 995 days between its first mission on August 17, 1942 and the German surrender on May 8, 1945, its planes had mounted ever-increasing attacks against Nazi airplane factories and airfields, oil refineries, submarine pens, railroads and water transportation networks, rocket-launching sites and many strategic and tactical targets. Tens of thousands of American, British and Russian lives were saved because bombing attacks by the Eighth Air Force prevented enemy submarines from being launched, planes from taking off, locomotives and trucks from having the fuel to haul supplies and ammunition for use against Allied troops.

In a letter to his wife near the end of hostilities, Doolittle reflected on what he had learned as a commander of the mightiest bombing force the world had ever known. He wrote:

"Command, regardless of its size or importance, carries with it both responsibility and opportunity. Responsibility to superiors and subordinates. Opportunity to utilize to advantage one's attributes and ability. It is difficult but necessary to exercise command in such a way as to assure the respect and loyalty of subordinates and the confidence of superiors. To strive to avoid engendering antagonism and annoyance and establish approbation, admiration and even affection. The last objective is rarely achieved, particularly among our contemporaries.

"I sometimes think that when all this is over I'd like to run a peanut stand. Would want it on a quiet street where there wouldn't be too many customers to interfere with my meditations. Actually, after about a week's rest, I imagine I'd be restless and looking for work and responsibility."

When the war in Europe came to a conclusion, Doolittle returned to the States and had a reunion with Joe and his sons Jim, Jr., and John, the latter a cadet at West Point. He learned that he would be moving the Eighth Air Force to the Pacific but first had to make a speaking tour to the west coast with General George S. Patton, fa-

While Lt. Gen. Doolittle laughs heartily, Gen. George Patton Jr., as much an actor as a fighter, mugs for the photographer at the generals' press conference. The famed military leaders were guests of the city during a two-day citywide homecoming celebration. Below the Los Angeles Coliseum filled for the generals' speeches. U.S. AIR FORCE PHOTOS

mous army hero whose ground forces had slashed across France and Germany. They gave speeches to factory workers to remind them that the war was not over. Doolittle then visited the Boeing factory to inspect and fly the B-29 Superfortress that the Eighth would be flying. He then flew one to Kadena Air Base on Okinawa via England, Egypt, India and the Philippines. The flag was raised at the new Eighth Air Force headquarters on July 26, 1945 as he prepared for the arrival of men and planes from the States.

On August 6, 1945, Colonel Paul W. Tibbetts, flying the *Enola Gay*, dropped the first atomic bomb on Hiroshima, Japan. When the Japanese refused to surrender after thousands of warning leaflets were dropped, the second atomic bomb was dropped on Nagasaki on August 9th. Meanwhile, the first two bomb groups of the Eighth arrived at Okinawa on the 7th. Word came from Washington that General Arnold wanted a 1,000-plane raid on Japan on August 8. The 20th Air Force was to put 850 bombers in the air; the Eighth would supply the rest. General Spaatz wired Jimmy that if he wanted to get into combat with the Japanese, he had better get his bombers into the air promptly. Doolittle refused. He wired back that he did not want to risk one airplane or the life of a single crew member just to be able to say that the Eighth Air Force had fought against both the Germans and the Japanese.

The Japanese surrendered on August 15, 1945 and the surrender ceremony was held on the battleship *Missouri.* Doolittle was there. He was relieved that the war was over and wondered what he would do next. He considered accepting a regular commission but turned it down. The Shell company wanted him back, not in his former position as head of the aviation depart-

Doolittle makes a radio address for his troops after arriving on Okinawa in the Pacific with the first complement of the Eighth Air Force in July 1945. A newsman sent him this photograph inscribed, "Brother, you'd better wear those glasses." DOOLITTLE COLLECTION, AIR FORCE ACADEMY ment but as a vice president. He would be a trouble-shooter and problem-solver. Doolittle accepted but had to ask for a concession to his acceptance.

"The air force is going to be a separate service one of these days," he told Shell officials, "and there are difficult days ahead as it tries to break away from the army and set up its own organization. I'm going to remain in the reserve and may be called back for various short-term assignments to help out. Will Shell go along with this possibility?"

Shell could and did. Jimmy shed the uniform in the fall of 1945 and moved to a plush office in New York City. One of his first voluntary tasks was to initiate the organization of the Air Force Association and accepted its first presidency. It wasn't long before he was called to serve the nation again. In 1946 he was asked to serve on the Secretary of War's Board on Officers/Enlisted Men Relationships. Known as the Doolittle Board, it had been formed because of complaints by World War II enlisted veterans of ill treatment by officers. The recommendations that the board made were highly controversial because old-time military officers thought they would result in a poorly disciplined military establishment.

Doolittle, fourth from left, was present on the battleship *Missouri* during the Japanese surrender ceremonies in Tokyo Bay on Sept. 2, 1945. Nearly 2,000 Navy and AAF bombers and fighters flew over afterward. DOOLITTLE COLLECTION

Controversial or not, the military services adopted most of the board's recommendations and Doolittle returned to his Shell office. However, he was soon called to serve on a Joint Congressional Aviation Policy Board, followed by appointment to a Committee on National Security Organization. These appointments were followed in later years by service on the Air Force Scientific Advisory Board, the President's Foreign Intelligence Advisory Board, and the National Advisory Committee for Aeronautics, the President's Science Advisory Committee, the Plowshare Committee of the Atomic Energy Commission, and similar groups that wanted his expertise and wise counsel.

John P. Doolittle was a cadet at the U.S. Military Academy and graduated in 1946. He completed flying training and served in Korea and later in the Strategic Air Command. DOOLITTLE COLLECTION

During his postwar years with Shell, he continued to fly a company-owned B-25 to make cross-country trips and test Shell fuels and lubricants in flight. To maintain familiarity with Air Force aircraft, he flew as co-pilot or observer in jet fighters and bombers. But after 40 years in the cockpit, Doolittle decided to quit flying as pilot altogether. "I decided this because I saw what happened to my friends who only half-quit," he told the author. "They flew less and less and didn't stay proficient. Inevitably they would be tempted to go into bad weather and they ended up dead. When I found that I could not fly enough to stay proficient, I decided to quit and I did."

Jimmy Doolittle may have decided to stop flying as a pilot but not as passenger. He traveled thousands of miles on the world's airlines as he hopped from place-to-place on Shell business, to give talks on maintaining a strong national defense or as a consultant to government and industry. He relaxed on hunting and fishing trips with old friends, including some of his Tokyo Raiders. He was an ardent conservationist and strongly sensitive to the effects of technology on the environment. He advocated strong laws to conserve the nation's natural resources or the planet would slowly destroy itself through wastefulness.

As he looked back over his busy life at age 90, he had developed a personal philosophy that guided him.

"My philosophy of life is really quite simple," he told the author. "I believe every person has been put on this earth for just one purpose: to serve his fellow man. It doesn't matter how he does this. He can build a bridge, paint a picture, invent a labor-saving gadget, or run a gas station. The point is, he should try to leave the earth a better place than he found it. If he does, his life will have been worthwhile. If he doesn't do what he can within his own limitations, he is destined to be unhappy."

Doolittle was a happy man. From the day he first tried to fly, he pursued each task and duty with the objective of doing something constructive to solve a problem or improve a situation. His career followed a pattern of purpose and consistence in which he never stopped trying to make the world he touched a better place for future generations.

He admitted, however, that there had been a bit of luck attached to his career as a flier. He crashed a number of times but always escaped unscathed. He never thought of himself as a bold, super-human pilot. "I have always tried to be conservative," he said. "I've always tried to do something new, but before exhibiting that new thing before the public, I practiced it again and again to be sure the hazard was minimized as much as possible. My calculations didn't always work out precisely, however. Otherwise, I wouldn't have had to jump out of an airplane three times to save my neck."

Doolittle formulated a set of values that he recommended, well realizing that he was a member of an older generation:

· Courage; physical and moral.
· Integrity; a man's word is his bond.
· Intelligence; a knowledge of things and people.

· Ambition; a willingness to strive mightily to attain our ends. A determination to progress—but not at the expense of others.

· Patriotism; to put Country above self.

· Humanity; love of people. Living by the Golden Rule.

· Spirituality; a realization that a universe as orderly as it is must be ruled by a Divine Purpose and not by the mind of man.

In one of his conversations with the author before his death, he said, "I am somewhat distressed to see a few of our young people abandon these values without coming up with something better in their place. I am not against change and I'm not against progress. I am for change as long as it represents progress. Every step that is taken should be a step forward."

Jimmy Doolittle's life was full of forward steps as he personally pushed back the frontiers of aeronautical knowledge. He was rewarded with a promotion to the four-star rank of General in the Air Force by Act of Congress in 1985; his fourth star was pinned on by President Ronald Reagan and former Senator Barry Goldwater.

He was invited to the White House again in 1989 where President George H. W. Bush presented him with the Presidential Medal of Freedom, the highest civilian award of our Government. He thus became the first American to receive both of the nation's most distinguished awards. The citation accompanying the Medal of Freedom expressed the feelings of a grateful nation:

"Aviation pioneer and military hero, James H. Doolittle is a symbol of vision and courage. His numerous contributions to aeronautical science, often at great personal hazard, extend from his earliest achievements in long-distance flying to the age of rockets. In the uniform of his country, General Doolittle's heroic leadership inspired the American people during the darkest hours of the Second World War. In public service, he continued to foster American advances in aeronautics, the cause to which he has devoted his life. For extraordinary service to his country, the American people salute one of their foremost heroes."

Jimmy's beloved wife Joe died on December 24, 1988, their 71st wedding anniversary, and was buried at Arlington National Cemetery. Jimmy died at age 96 on September 27, 1993 and is buried with her.

President Harry S. Truman signs legislation establishing the U.S. Air Force in 1947. Looking on are Doolittle, Gen. Hoyt S.Vandenberg, Air Force Vice Chief of Staff; Lauris Norstad, Director of Plans and Operations, and Stuart Symington, the first Secretary of the Air Force.
U.S. AIR FORCE PHOTO

Doolittle (on left) and other famous pilots received the International Harmon Trophy from President Harry S. Truman in 1949. It is one of several personal trophies given for achievements in aerial flight awarded from a grant established by Col. Clifford B. Harmon (1866-1945), pioneer balloonist and aviator, since 1926. The awards were suspended during World War II and given retroactively.
DOOLITTLE COLLECTION, AIR FORCE ACADEMY

President Harry S. Truman explains to Doolittle the reasons he asked him to head a special commission to study civilian aircraft accidents and crowded airports. The report, titled "The Airport and Its Neighbors," was issued in 1952 and led to a number of air safety improvements and recommendations for the future. ASSOCIATED PRESS PHOTO

President Truman presents the Wright Brothers Memorial Trophy to Doolittle in December 1952. It was awarded for his "significant public service of enduring value to aviation in the United States." U.S. AIR FORCE PHOTO

Actor Jimmy Stewart (l), Gen. Carl "Tooey" Spaatz and Doolittle were three of the leaders in the establishment of the Air Force Association after World War II. Stewart had served as operations officer in an Eighth Air Force B-24 bomb group in Europe and retired from the Air Force reserve as a brigadier general. DOOLITTLE COLLECTION, AIR FORCE ACADEMY

Doolittle served on a number of federal boards and commissions in the post-World War II years. One of these was the President's Foreign Intelligence Board shown here with board members and President John F. Kennedy. WHITE HOUSE PHOTO

President Lyndon B. Johnson called on Doolittle (at far left end of table) to head a defense committee in 1964 chaired by Clark Clifford (left). WHITE HOUSE PHOTO

Air Line Pilots Association president John J. O'Donnell presents a plaque to Jimmy Doolittle that designates him an Honorary Air Line Pilot for his contributions to aviation safety and progress. Only one other pilot - Charles A. Lindbergh - has been so honored. AIR LINE PILOTS ASSOCIATION PHOTO

Doolittle served on the board of directors of Thompson-Ramo-Wooldridge (TRW) for six years beginning in 1953, then was named chairman of the board of Space Technology Laboratories (STL), a subsidiary, in 1959. STL PHOTO

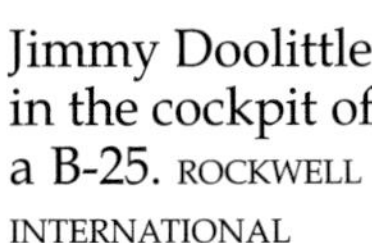

Jimmy Doolittle in the cockpit of a B-25. ROCKWELL INTERNATIONAL

Doolittle and former South Dakota Governor Joe Foss proudly hold the salmon they caught off Westport, Washington in 1970. The occasion was an informal meeting of five Medal of Honor recipients. Foss was awarded the medal for his World War II exploits in the South Pacific and was the Marine Corps' top fighter ace. ASSOCIATED PRESS PHOTO

Syndicated columnist Bob Considine, master of ceremonies, congratulates Doolittle for being designated an Honorary Air Line Pilot after a humorous 1971 dinner in Washington, D.C. An enlarged photograph was supplied to satisfy the requirement that a photograph had to accompany such a nomination. Doolittle commented that it proved that he did have hair at one time. AIR LINE PILOTS ASSOCIATION PHOTO

Spencer Tracy played Lieutenant Colonel Doolittle in the movie, *Thirty Seconds Over Tokyo*, at his own request. "It is a great honor to portray one of America's great heroes," Tracy said.

GRATIFYING AMENDMENT

Appendix

Career Summary

U.S. Army Air Service and Air Corps, 1917-1930
Major, U.S. Army Air Corps Reserve, 1930-1940
Major, U.S. Army Air Corps, 1940
Lieutenant Colonel, 1942
Brigadier General, 1942
Major General, 1942
Lieutenant General, 1944
General, 1985
Commanding General, 12th Air Force, North Africa, 1942
Commanding General, 15th Air Force, Italy, 1943
Commanding General, 8th Air Force, England, 1944
Commanding General, 8th Air Force, Okinawa, 1945
Vice President, Shell Union Oil Co., 1946-1947
Director, Shell Union Oil Co., 1946-1967
Chairman of the Board, Space Technology Laboratories, 1959-1962
Director, Space Technology Laboratories, 1959-1963
Director, Thompson-Ramo-Wooldridge Co., 1961-1969
Consultant, TRW Systems, 1962-1965
Director, Mutual of Omaha Insurance Co., 1961-1986
Director Emeritus and Consultant, Mutual of Omaha Insurance Co., 1986-1990
Trustee, Aerospace Corporation, 1963-1969
Vice Chairman, Board of Trustees, and Chairman of Executive Committee, Aerospace Corporation, 1965-1969
Director, United Benefit Life Insurance Co. of Omaha, 1964-1980
Director, Tele-Trip Co., 1966-1980
Director, Companion Life Insurance Co. of New York, 1968-1980
Director, Mutual of Omaha Growth & Income Funds, 1968-1980

Military Decorations

Medal of Honor
Distinguished Service Medal, with Oak Leaf Cluster
Silver Star
Distinguished Flying Cross, with two Oak Leaf Clusters
Bronze Star
Air Medal, with three Oak Leaf Clusters
Order of the Condor (Bolivia)
Yon-Hwei, Class III (China)
Knight Commander, Order of the Bath (Great Britain)
Grand Officer of the Legion d'Honneur and Croix de Guerre, with Palm (France)
Grand Order of the Crown, with Palm, and Croix de Guerre with Palm (Belgium)
Grand Commander (Poland)
Abdon Calderon, First Class (Ecuador)

Honors and Awards

Schneider Marine Cup, 1925
Mackay Trophy, 1925
Spirit of St. Louis Award, 1929
Harmon Trophy, Ligue des Aviateurs, 1930
Bendix Trophy, 1931
Thompson Trophy, 1932
Guggenheim Trophy, 1942
International Harmon Trophy, 1940, 1949
Wright Brothers Trophy, 1953
Federation Aeronautique Internationale Gold Medal, 1954
Silver Quill, 1959
International Aerospace Hall of Fame, San Diego, California, 1966
Aviation Hall of Fame, Dayton, Ohio, 1967
Thomas D. White National Defense Award, 1967
Horatio Alger Award, 1972
Conservation Hall of Fame, 1973
Wings of Man Award, Society of Experimental Test Pilots, 1973
Bishop Wright Air Industry Award, 1975
Sylvanus Thayer Award, U.S. Military Academy, 1983
C.C. Criss Award, 1984
Motorsports Hall of Fame Award, 1989
Grand Cross of Honour, Supreme Council of Scottish Rite, 1989
Presidential Medal of Freedom, 1989

Education

Manual Arts High School, Los Angeles, California
Los Angeles Junior College, 1916-1917
University of California, Bachelor of Arts, 1922
Massachusetts Institute of Technology, Master of Science, 1924 and Doctor of Science, 1925

Bibliography

Arnold, Henry H., *Global Mission*. New York: Harper and Brothers, 1949.

Cohen, Stan, *Destination Tokyo, A Pictorial History of Doolittle's Tokyo Raid, April 18, 1942.* Missoula, Montana: Pictorial Histories Publishing Co., 1983.

Doolittle, James H., *I Could Never Be So Lucky Again*. New York: Bantam Books, 1991.

Emmens, Robert G., *Guests of the Kremlin*. New York: The Macmillan Company, 1949.

Freeman, Roger A., *The Mighty Eighth: A History of the U.S. 8th Air Force.* Garden City, New York: Doubleday & Co., 1970.

Glines, Carroll V., *Doolittle's Tokyo Raiders.* Princeton, New Jersey: D. Van Nostrand Co., 1964.

Glines, Carroll V., *Four Came Home, The Gripping Story of the Survivors of Jimmy Doolittle's Two Lost Crews*. Missoula, Montana: Pictorial Histories Publishing Co., 1995.

Glines, Carroll V., *The Doolittle Raid: America's First Strike Against Japan.* Atglen, Pennsylvania: Schiffer Publishing, Ltd., 1991.

Glines, Carroll V., *The Compact History of the U. S. Air Force.* New York: Hawthorn Books, 1973.

Hallion, Richard P., *Legacy of Flight: The Guggenheim Contribution to American Aviation.* Seattle, Washington: University of Washington Press, 1977.

Thomas, Lowell and Edward Jablonski, *Doolittle: A Biography.* Garden City, New York: Doubleday and Co., 1976.

Brig. Gen. Jimmy Doolittle pictured in 1942. U.S. AIR FORCE PHOTO

The Doolittle Library display at the University of Texas, Dallas. PHOTO BY THE AUTHOR

Doolittle Tokyo Raiders exhibit and B-25 at the Hill Aerospace Museum, Hill Air Force Base, Utah. HILL AIR FORCE BASE PUBLIC AFFAIRS OFFICE

Doolittle Tokyo Raiders exhibit at the Strategic Air & Space Museum in Ashland, Nebraska. PHOTO COURTESY BRIAN YORK

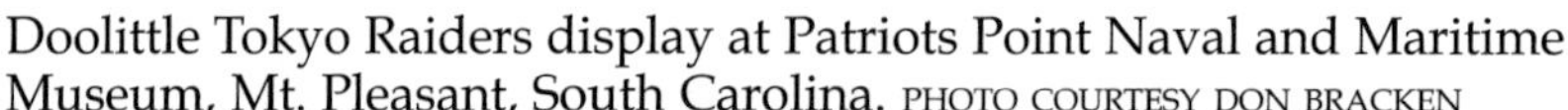

Doolittle Tokyo Raiders display at Patriots Point Naval and Maritime Museum, Mt. Pleasant, South Carolina. PHOTO COURTESY DON BRACKEN

The B-25 display and the Doolittle Raiders display at the U.S. Air Force Musem, Wright-Patterson Air Force Base, Dayton, Ohio. WPAFB PUBLIC AFFAIRS OFFICE

Doolittle Tokyo Raiders display at the Smithsonian National Air and Space Museum, Washington, D.C.

The Travis Historical Society/ Jimmy Doolittle Air & Space Museum Foundation is raising money for their museum at Travis Air Force Base, California (as of 2002). The Nome City Council in Alaska (as of 2002) is considering renaming their airport after Jimmy Doolittle.

The Doolittle Tokyo Raiders display at the Admiral Nimitz State Historic Site/The National Museum of the Pacific War, Fredericksburg, Texas. PHOTO COURESTY SHIRLEY WILLS

About the Author

Carroll V. Glines is a retired Air Force colonel and command pilot. A graduate with master's degrees from the University of Oklahoma and American University, he began writing professionally on a free lance basis while in the service and is the author of 34 books and more than 750 articles for national magazines. After retirement from the Air Force, he was successively an associate editor for *Armed Forces Management* and editor of *Air Cargo, Air Line Pilot*, and *Professional Pilot* magazines. He has been listed in Who's Who in America since 1976 and has won writing awards from the Freedoms Foundation, Aviation/Space Writers Association, Alaska Press Association, International Association of Business Communicators and International Labor Press Association. He was awarded the Max Steinbock Award in 1981 for "Humanistic Spirit in Journalism" and the prestigious Lauren D. Lyman Award in 1984 for "Outstanding achievement in aviation writing." He resides in Dallas, Texas and has been a curator for the Doolittle Library at the University of Texas at Dallas since 1994.

Photo taken April 1967 at Doolittle Raiders reunion in Alameda, California, (left to right) Robert Hite, author C.V. Glines, George Barr, Jacob DeShazer and Chase Nielsen. Barr passed away in July 1967. These were the Raiders who survived 40 months as prisoners of the Japanese.

Doolittle and the author tour the National Air & Space Museum together in 1990 where Doolittle's exploits are featured in several displays. The aircraft he flew in the 1925 Schneider Cup Race is located on the second floor. HENRY GASQUE PHOTO

About the Cover Artists

Jean Bolefahr Pilk

Jean Bolefahr Pilk's portrait of General Doolittle hangs in the Scottish Rite Hall of Honor in Washington, D.C. She has been hailed as one of America's premier portrait artists and the *Los Angeles Times* listed her among the top four portrait artists in the country, the only woman among them. She has been awarded commissions for members of the U.S. Cabinet, Armed Forces and Congressional leaders, as well as the officers and directors of leading U.S. corporations and associations. Pilk lives in Aiken, South Carolina with her husband, Jack. Her web site is www.jeanpilkportraits.com

John D. Shaw

John D. Shaw has pursued his art and graphics career since 1985. Born in 1961, this native of Carson City, Nevada has always maintained an interest in creating both fine and commercial art. As an illustrator, Shaw has created artwork for a variety of clients such as Lucasfilms Ltd., Kellogg's, Major League Baseball and Coast Federal Bank of California.

Shaw's work took a major new emphasis in 1993, when he began creating paintings with an historical aviation theme. With special attention to the World War II era, his depictions of these aircraft, people and their missions have won national awards and have illustrated a number of related national publications, such as *Flying, Aviation History, World War II* and *Military History*.

To date, 13 of these paintings have been reproduced as limited-edition lithographs, all of which are hand-signed by Shaw and famous aviators such as Chennault's Flying Tigers, the Doolittle Tokyo Raiders, Black Sheep Squadron, Tuskegee Airmen, Mercury Astronauts and others.

Shaw's most recent effort, the world's highest scoring living fighter ace, General Gunther Rall of Germany was reunited with the highest scoring living American ace, Col. Francis 'Gabby" Gabreski and other prominent pilots of the famed 56th Fighter Group (better known as 'Zemke's Wolfpack'), in a scene depicting the 1944 mission in which Rall was shot down by the Wolfpack, losing his left thumb and nearly his life.

Now long-time friends with his former adversaries, Rall's long-awaited biography was released in March 2002 and features Shaw's painting and illustrations throughout.

More information about Shaw's work can be obtained through:

Liberty Studios
321 Secret Way Court
Casselberry, Florida 32707
Phone (888) 893-3786
Fax (407) 265-0260.

Acknowledgments

During the past 40 years I have researched the life and contributions of Jimmy Doolittle for a biography and later as co-author of his autobiography. I also wrote a number of articles and three books about the famous air mission against Japan that he led in April 1942. I interviewed him on many occasions at his home, in Washington and various cities during reunions of his Tokyo Raiders. No writer could have better cooperation from an interviewee that I did during the many interesting question-and-answer sessions.

I am especially indebted to John P. Doolittle, Jimmy's youngest son, and his devoted wife Priscilla for their hospitality during my visits and their unending efforts to locate background materials when questions arose. The scrapbooks compiled by Mrs. Doolittle, now in the National Archives, provided news clippings and correspondence about her husband's many news-making experiences during his flying years. His own voluminous correspondence files, now in the McDermott Library of the University of Texas at Dallas, provided valuable information about his life after retirement from the Air Force.

Jimmy Doolittle may have had more photographs taken of him during his busy lifetime than any other aviator. When his active flying days were over, he continued to make history as a counselor and advisor to presidents, government agencies, especially the Air Force, and the aerospace industry. He traveled extensively and was photographed wherever he went. Copies of many of these prints were sent to him for his files. During his final years, he sent hundreds of them to the Air Force Academy for the use of future researchers.

I am especially indebted to Duane J. Reed, guardian of the Academy's Special Collections, for his assistance in providing the albums for research and arranging for the copying of those I selected for this book. Other photo sources include the National Archives, National Air & Space Museum, Air Force files and individuals who knew, served with, or worked with him during his lifetime.

It was the privilege of a lifetime to know and work with Jimmy Doolittle, a man of integrity, honesty and accomplishment. When I asked if he had a philosophy that guided him during his life, he answered: "I believe we were all put here on this earth with just one purpose - to served our fellow man. It doesn't matter what form this service takes. You can build a bridge or write a poem or paint a picture or have a house by the side of the road for the weary traveler. The criterion is this - if a man leaves the earth a better place than he found it, then his life has been worthwhile."

I hope readers of this book will agree that Jimmy Doolittle has left the earth a better place than he found it.

The Doolittles pose for the camera in their Santa Monica, California home which featured the big game hunting trophies and plaques awarded over a lifetime. They lived there until 1978 when they moved to Carmel, California. Doolittle was an ardent conservationist and sportsman who was resolutely against poachers and law-breakers.
DOOLITTLE COLLECTION, AIR FORCE ACADEMY

Doolittle's favorite way of relaxing was hunting and fishing. Here he displays his catch of the day in November 1986 with four of his Tokyo Raiders who shared his outdoor interests: (l to r) Robert L. Hite, William M. Bower, Doolittle, Richard A. Knobloch and Richard E. Cole. DOOLITTLE COLLECTION, AIR FORCE ACADEMY

A happy fisherman displays a large trout he caught on one of his many fishing trips. He delighted in cooking his catches over a camp fire.
DOOLITTLE COLLECTION, AIR FORCE ACADEMY

A smiling Doolittle has his fourth stars pinned on by President Reagan and Senator Barry Goldwater in 1985 ceremonies at the White House. The legislation authorizing the unprecedented promotion to be made to a reserve officer had been introduced by Goldwater. No other reservist has ever held three- or four-star rank.
WHITE HOUSE PHOTO

"Joe" and Jimmy Doolittle receive prestigious C.C. Criss Awards from Bob and Delores Hope in 1984 at a Hollywood ceremony attended by movie stars and political dignitaries. The award was given to honor outstanding contributions to health, safety, education, and/or public welfare. Delores Hope stated that "Joe" Doolittle had shared her courage with women everywhere and therefore deserved an award of her own.
DOOLITTLE COLLECTION

President and Mrs. George H.W. Bush congratulate Doolittle as he received the Presidential Medal of Freedom in July 1989. No other person had ever received this award in addition to the Medal of Honor. WHITE HOUSE PHOTO

The two General Jimmys pose for the cameras during a Tokyo Raider reunion in Carmel, California. Brig. Gen. Jimmy Stewart was the only major motion picture star to complete AAF pilot training and fly in combat. PHOTO BY THE AUTHOR

Dedication of the new Air Force Association National Headquarters building in Arlington, Virginia, September 16, 1984. Left to right: Pennsylvania Superior Court Judge John G. Brosky, Chairman of the Board of Directors, National Air Force Association; William E. Brooks, past president Air Force Association and delegate to the National Air Force Association Convention; Doolittle; bust of General Doolittle and the sculptor of the bust. PICTORIAL HISTORIES PUBLISHING COMPANY COLLECTION

The casket bearing the body of General Doolittle was flown from California on an Air Force transport for burial at Arlington National Cemetery with his beloved "Joe." His funeral on October 1, 1993, was attended by hundreds of family, friends and men who served under him during World War II, including his Tokyo Raiders. U.S. AIR FORCE PHOTO

Memorial procession for General J.H. Doolittle at Fort Myer Memorial Chapel, October 1, 1993.
DOOLITTLE LIBRARY, UNIVERSITY OF TEXAS, DALLAS

At left, this bronze sculpture of Doolittle is on display at the University of Texas, Dallas.

This Doolittle Raiders monument was placed at the U.S. Air Force Museum in Dayton, Ohio, in 1988.

ALL PHOTOS BY THE AUTHOR

The headstone of Jimmy and Joe at Arlington National Cemetery. They are buried together. His inscription is on the front and Joe's is on the back of the same stone.

COLLECTIBLES

1932

1942

Bubble gum cards.

1944

1942

First Bombing of Tokyo The Japanese couldn't believe it—till the bombs fell—but the Americans *had* bombed Tokyo! With superb skill, Jimmy Doolittle did what had never been done before—flew long-range bombers from the deck of a carrier at sea. Into the heart of Japan they flew, bearing the first of the thousands of tons of bombs to hit Japan. With superb Navy seamanship, and great Army flying, the job that "couldn't be done" *was* done on April 18, 1942, scarcely more than 4 months after Pearl Harbor.

Coral Sea The Japanese were ready to advance into Southeast New Guinea, and began to concentrate ships for the push. In May, 1942, the first American task force contact was made, surprising and all but destroying 12 warships and transports at Tulagi. Three days later, planes from 3 U.S. carriers found a large Japanese force in the Coral Sea, and sank one carrier, and four cruisers, plusotherships. The old carrier Lexington was wounded and was lost because of internal explosions.

First in battle at the Coral Sea, and then at Midway, the Grumman TBF Avenger is a versatile torpedo bomber that can operate either from a carrier or land base.

Kellogg's cereal box card.

Poster.

World War II game.

A TRIBUTE TO
GENERAL JAMES H. "JIMMY" DOOLITTLE
FROM
HIS TOKYO RAIDERS

Our leader has fallen.

He led us in peace and in war. And he led us by example.

He was an uncommon man whose foresight, integrity, courage and intellect are unmatched in the annals of aviation. He was a man of wisdom and wit, compassion and concern. His extraordinary feats in an airplane were matched by his ability to command men from the smallest units, such as the 79 of us who participated with him in our raid on Japan, to the 8th Air Force, the largest aerial fighting force in history. He was a patriot in the fullest sense of the word.

We called him "Boss" and referred to him as "The Old Man" which were titles of respect for the man who formed our group, trained us to his high standards and led us off the carrier in the first attack against a nation half way around the world that had been foresworn to take away our freedoms. It was considered an impossible task because never before had a fully-loaded, land-based bomber been launched from a Navy carrier. He knew it was possible but we weren't so sure. His ability to analyze and verify before performing seemingly impossible feats had earned him the title of "Master of the Calculated Risk." His "can do" spirit was contagious and we followed.

Our leader's spirit lives on in the hearts of his Tokyo Raiders and their families. He considered us members of his family with all the pride of love and camaraderie that this implies.

Yes, our leader has fallen and he will rest forever in a hallowed place with his comrades-in-arms. All Americans should be proud that he walked among us. We of his Tokyo Raiders are grateful that we were privileged to serve with him.

WRITTEN BY C.V. GLINES FOR THE RAIDERS AND READ BY DAVY JONES AT THE GENERAL'S FUNERAL AT ARLINGTON CEMETERY.